CW01011081

Public List

VIEW FROM THE MAIN GATE. Taken from rebel photographs of the prison when it contained thirty-five thousand men. Original picture in possession of the author.

MARTYRIA;

OR,

ANDERSONVILLE PRISON.

BY

AUGUSTUS C. HAMLIN,

LATE MEDICAL INSPECTOR U. S. ARMY, ROYAL ANTIQUARIAN, ETC.

Illustrated by the Author.

BOSTON:

LEE AND SHEPARD.

1866.

Cambridge Press
DAKIN AND METCALF.

STEREOTYPED AT THE
BOSTON STEREOTYPE FOUNDRY,

TO THE

MEMORY OF THE MEN

WHO STEADILY UPHELD THE CAUSE OF CIVIL LIBERTY,

AND

WHO PREFERRED LINGERING DEATH,

IN THE MIDST OF UNPARALLELED PRIVATIONS
AND HORRORS,

RATHER THAN DISHONOR

AND DENIAL OF THEIR BIRTHRIGHTS,

THIS BOOK

IS RESPECTFULLY INSCRIBED.

NOTE.

THE author presents for review neither style nor language: he offers simply the story of the wrong and the heroism, the cause and effect, as it rises in his mind.

Neither does he, at this late date, seek to rekindle the smouldering embers of hate and conflict, nor, Antony-like, attack persons under the recital of the wrongs. Vengeance does not belong to the human race. There are times in the history of men when human invectives are without force. "There are deeds of which men are no judges, and which mount, without appeal, direct to the tribunal of God."

AUGUSTUS CHOATE HAMLIN.

BANGOR, September, 1866.

MARTYRIA.

<blockquote>
" They never fail who die
In a great cause.   *   *   *   *
They but augment the deep and sweeping thoughts
Which overpower all others, and conduct
The world at last to freedom."
</blockquote>

Byron.

I.

HISTORY weighs the social institutions of men in the scale of Humanity. Time, slowly but surely, accumulates the evidence which relates to their materials. It calmly but firmly unveils the statues which men erect as their principles, and with " that retributive justice which God has implanted in our very acts, as a conscience more sacred than the fatalism of the ancients," lays bare the secret springs of action which have prompted the deeds of heroism or baseness, of virtue or crime.

Nations are political institutions, and like the system of nature, which is governed by positive and fixed laws, so they likewise are swayed and directed by mysterious forces, and influenced and moulded into form by those external circumstances which are greatly within the control of man. Their rise and decadence is in direct ratio to the nature and integrity of their customs, the structure of their social fabrics, the vigor of the spirit of independence which animates their thoughts, or the strength of the despotism which consumes their vitals. "Liberty brings benedictions in spite of nature, and in defiance of the same nature tyranny brings maledictions. Slavery has always produced only villany, vice, and misery."

Men cannot perpetuate a creed or a system that is not founded on the eternal principles of justice and virtue, no more than they can control the elements — no more than they can remove or obliterate those geographical boundaries, beyond which the human races cannot pass in pursuit of the forms of wealth or the dreams of ambition.

The Belgian, who has studied so long and so faithfully the laws of metaphysics, exclaims, " All those things which appear to be left to the free will, the passions, or the degree of intelligence of men, are regulated by laws as fixed, immutable, and eternal as those which govern the phenomena of the natural world! "

II.

Along the southern tier of the great States which form the American Republic, whose gigantic structure and almost supernatural vigor already overshadow and animate the older civilizations of the world, we observe vast extents of level and alluvial lands and deltas, or "rather a series of littoral bands of remarkable disposition," which the ocean left when receding from the mountain shores of the interior to its present limits, or which slowly and gradually emerged from their watery bed in the upheavals during the long intervals of the earth's ages.

This immense territory, stretching from the Potomac to the Rio Grande, and hardly broken throughout this long distance by undulations of the soil, embraces more than six hundred thousand square miles — an extent greater than that of France and the States of the Germanic Confederation combined. Eight millions of human souls inhabit the one, whilst one hundred millions people the other. Ignorance and brutality darken the one, intelligence and humanity illuminate the other.

III.

The proximity of the sea, the configuration of the soil, the presence or absence of mountains, affect the growth and character of nations, and leave their impress upon their institutions. Climate and purity of blood complete the determination in the problem of life, the progress, and degree of development. Upon these

1 *

external causes also depend, in a great measure, the vigor of the imagination, the sentiment of the grand and the beautiful, the vivacity and purity of the soul.

The cold breezes of the temperate zones conduce men to wisdom, reason, and philosophy. The enervating atmospheres of hot climes incline the mind and body to repose, and often pervert the notions of natural justice. In the one, the mind is ever delighted and refreshed by the varying scenes of nature ; in the other, the forms of the mournful and the terrible alone excite the imagination.

IV.

We have seen these lands occupied for more than two centuries by the emigrants from European countries ; we have seen the reckless adventurer, the noble exile, the fugitive from justice, the outcast of society, blended together here in the experiment of colonization.

The form is still the same, for form is always more persistent than material in organic life, but the sterling and generous qualities of the primitive stock have greatly changed.

We have seen in these lands Slavery — that relic of barbarism, that leprosy, the foulest that ever preyed upon the vitals of any state — transplanted by that accursed Dutch ship, under the guise of Humanity, flourish, increase, and assume, during this brief period, the proportions of a despotism so powerful, so tenacious, as to defy and resist, almost successfully, the entire strength and resources of the Republic, enriching the slave faction with enormous wealth, but debasing and deteriorating the morals, the blood of the poor and neiest, the holding whites.   ntion,

This increase of three millions of black men weed held in bondage as human cattle by a few thousand white men. To these unfortunate creatures society extended no generosity, no consideration, but what reduced them still lower in the scale of organized beings, and chained them more closely in the sordid and selfish interests of their remorseless masters. To teach the black man to read, even the light of the divine Gospel, was a matter of fine, and imprisonment, and sometimes death.

v.

Seeking to perpetuate this atrocious system, this right of brute force over the helpless black, and establish a despotism with Slavery as its basis, the arrogant faction boldly took up arms against the Republic. " When Fortune," says the Latin historian, " is determined upon the ruin of a people, she can so blind them as to render them insensible to danger, even of the greatest magnitude."

Their appeals to arms were in the name of justice and glory, but they were without the echo of liberty and humanity. They summoned the masses of poor whites, whom they had degraded below the level of the slave, to rise and fight for their liberties, which were as empty as the winds of the desert. There were no liberties, no privileges for the poor whites, but to curse poverty and question God's providence.

The individual desires of the few had usurped and

external ed up the rights of society. There was no so-
vigor but the relation between the black man and his
and ster. The law, order, and force were all within the
control of the rich slaveholder.

The masses were either their tools, or too abject to
be considered as dangerous; too ignorant to be feared
as seditious, too poor to be regarded as anything more
than trash, below the level and the value of the negro.
This condition of the poor whites was the result of
physical, political, and moral causes, long and silently
at work.

VI.

The pretence for strife was resistance to oppression,
and the extension and perfection of liberty to the masses;
yet they impelled the people to passion, without mingling
a single truth with the illusions with which they decorated
their standards. Whilst they talked of the independent
spirit of the new government, and the glory of resisting
the oppressive policy of the invaders, every act and edict
gathered closer and stronger the bonds which degraded
and burdened the poor white.

The owner of seven slaves was exempt from the hazard
of battle, but poverty and starvation of family were no
causes of exemption for the non-slaveholder.

The real design, concealed by the strife, was the foundation of an empire of gigantic and seductive form,
radiant and glittering with the splendid architecture of
aristocratic sovereignty, but without reason or conscience.

The resolve was to control the production of the principal staples of industry and trade, and subject the commercial world to their caprices.

Thus they preferred the intoxications of conquest, the gratifications of lust, to the triumphs of true civilization, o the congratulations of a redeemed race. They cared not for reputation among the nations of the earth, nor immortality, nor renown; and they neglected or despised those happy stars which, now and then, conduct men and races to glory. "Glory belongs to the God in heaven; upon the earth it is the lot of virtue, and not of genius — of that virtue which is useful, grand, beneficent, brilliant, heroic."

VII.

Revolutions almost always spring from the noble and generous enthusiasm of youth; but seditions arise from the vulgar and ignoble crowd, or from the outcast few, who would, for wealth, sacrifice all that honor and nature hold dear; or for the meaner gratifications of self-aggrandizement, would crumble into dust, and scatter to the winds of the earth, the noblest institutions and laws of mankind. Who will say that this resort to arms was an insurrection of justice in favor of the weak, or that it was a revolt of nature against tyranny?

The agitations of revolutions stir up the innermost natures of men, and from the revelations out of the depths appear the extreme qualities of the soul, elevated or debased, according to the inspirations from Heaven or the influence of a vile cause.

What rays of intellectual light, what flashes of genuine eloquence, burst forth during the tempestuous times of this period to illumine their progress or define the glory of their future? When the minds and imaginations of men are moved in civil war, they betray, in spite of themselves, the nobility or meanness of their cause. Even the ignorant, says Quintilian, when moved by the violent passions, do not seek for what they are to say. It is the soul alone that renders them eloquent. Only the hoarse clamors for revenge, or the hollow laugh against the remonstrance of humanity, do we hear from their tribunals and halls of legislation. Fatuity possessed their minds, and rather than not succeed in their designs, the leaders would have preferred a dreary solitude to the best interests of humanity, or, like Erostratus, they would have rather burned down the temple of liberty itself.

"Pejus deteriusque tyrannide sive injusto imperio, bellum civile."

VIII.

Civil liberty is again triumphant, but at what a sacrifice of human life! What a deluge of blood has been poured over nature's fields, where the contending armies have struggled together! A half a million of lives have been yielded up in this the nation's sacrifice.

"The tree of Liberty," said Barere, "is best watered with the blood of tyrants;" but how few among this immense host of victims were the originators of the sedition! The merciless schemers of bloody and cruel wars rarely expose their precious lives to the chances of combat.

During the existence of the slave system, and the long period of its progress, what has it produced to enrich the heritage of the human mind? Where are the holy and pure traditions, the bright recollections?

Neither wisdom nor philosophy has appeared, nor those arts which serve to form the "happy genius of nations." There are countries where the march of ideas is accelerated only by the force of selfish passions; and philanthropy, that true index of civilization, only appears when it is required by mercantilism or political ambition. The aims and influences of commercial and political life can debase and destroy the noblest impulses. "It is a grand and beautiful spectacle," exclaims the eloquent Rousseau, "to see man issue forth out of nothingness, as it were, by his own proper efforts, to dissipate, by the light of his reason, the shadows in which nature had enveloped him, to elevate himself even above himself, to glance with his spirit even into the celestial regions, to pass, with the stride of a giant, even as the sun, through the vast expanse of the universe, and what is still greater and more difficult, to enter one's self, and study there man, and to understand his nature, his duties, and his end."

IX.

Civilization claims to introduce the elements of peace, happiness, and prosperity into the structure of society, and to transform the sword and the spear into the harmless implements of husbandry; yet with a swifter pace the engines of war increase, man thirsts as fiercely for the blood of his fellow-man, and the dormant spirit of destruction is as ready to illume the torch, as in the reckless times of past history. Even in this enlightened age we are constantly reminded of the truth and force of the remark of Hannibal: "No great state can long remain at rest. If it has no enemies abroad, it finds them at home ; as overgrown bodies seem safe from external injuries, but suffer grievous inconveniences from their own strength."

The motives of self-aggrandizement by force of arms appear to be innate in human nature. We see men maintaining monstrous ideas. We see great armies singularly swayed by single minds, in defiance of truth and reason. The soldiers of Catiline fought to the last gasp, and perished to a man, embracing the eagle of Marius — "Marius, who sprang from the dust the expiring Gracchi flung towards heaven," and who first dared attack the aristocratic nobility, and defend the down-trodden rights of the oppressed plebeian. There are mysterious laws, which seem to regulate the expansion and the decay of the human families. There are unseen forces which now and then impel vicious men to their own destruction.

X.

ANDERSONVILLE — a name which has been stamped so deeply by cruelty into the pages of American history — is one of those miserable little hamlets, of a score of scattered and dilapidated farm-houses, which relieve the monotony of the wide and dreary level of sand plains, which, covered with immense forests, interspersed with fens, marshes, corn and cotton fields, stretch away, in unbroken surface, from Macon down to the Florida shores. The plantations, which were tilled by slave labor, are almost concealed in the recesses of the forests, so thickly wooded is the country. Here and there only, where the savannas are of unusual fertility, do the cleared lands

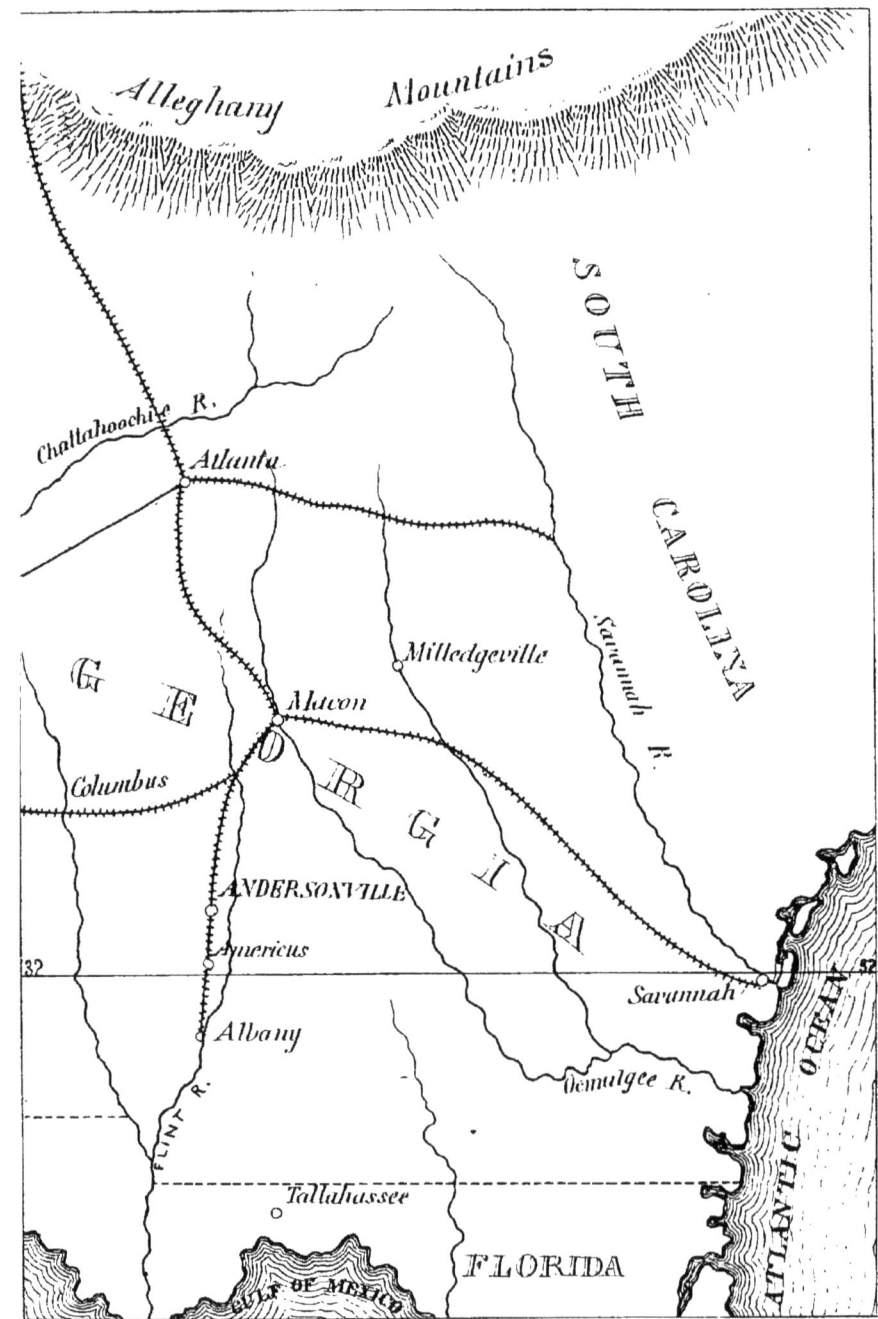

give a wide and extended view of the landscape, but the primeval pines everywhere hide the distant horizon.

The song of the laborer rarely disturbs the silence, which is oppressive. Song is the impulsive outburst of a heart filled with joy and hope. The slave has neither. His voice is the cry of anguish, of a soul burdened and crushed, and is more like the moan of the winds than the accents of civilized man.

The physical aspect of the white inhabitant indicates the local impressions and inspirations — listless and apathetic in look, lank and haggard in form. There are countries, there are even limited localities, where the moral and mental faculties expand in accordance with external impressions. The laws of beauty and deformity are regulated by the condition and circumstances of the outward world to a remarkable degree.

The landscape, the sunshine, and the luxuriance at Corinth and Athens gave rise to the most beautiful flowers of art and love, and to that wonderful type of human beauty, which the world has since lost; but the rugged and stern defiles of the mountains of Calabria, of Albania, and the dreary marsh fens of the Campagna, or of the Netherlands, still produce characters that rival in ferocity the hyenas of the desert.

*   *   *   *

Nature appears to have selected for man the sites where are performed the noble acts which charm and enlighten the mind, or the dark deeds which cause men to ponder and regret the frailty of their organization. " It seems that the instincts of war conduct from age to age the armies of successive empires to the same rendezvous of contest, and that geography has laid off in advance certain fields of battle, as a sort of arena for these great immolations of humanity." " Hungary," said Sobieski, " is a clump of earth, which, if squeezed, would give out but human blood." The name and look of Andersonville will always be synonymous with and suggestive of cruelty.

XI.

At the distance of eight hundred paces from the railway which connects the town with Central Georgia on the north and the Gulf of Mexico on the south, appears the Prison Stockade, which was located by the Winders of the Rebel army, at the suggestion of Howell Cobb, in 1863, and occupied for its specific purpose in February, 1864.

It is situated about fifty miles south of Macon, and its position on the geographical map is defined by longitude $7°$ $30'$ west from Washington, latitude $32°$ $10'$ north of the equator, corresponding in the western hemisphere to the central region of Algiers.

A dense forest of primeval trees covered the spot which was selected by the engineers when they marked out the line of the prison. The massive pines were levelled by the strong arms of several hundred negro slaves, and when their branches were cut away, they were placed side by side, standing upright in the deep ditches, which were excavated with regularity, and in parallel lines, north and south, east and west. Thus were formed the boundaries of the palisade, wherein nearly forty thousand human beings were to be herded at one time.

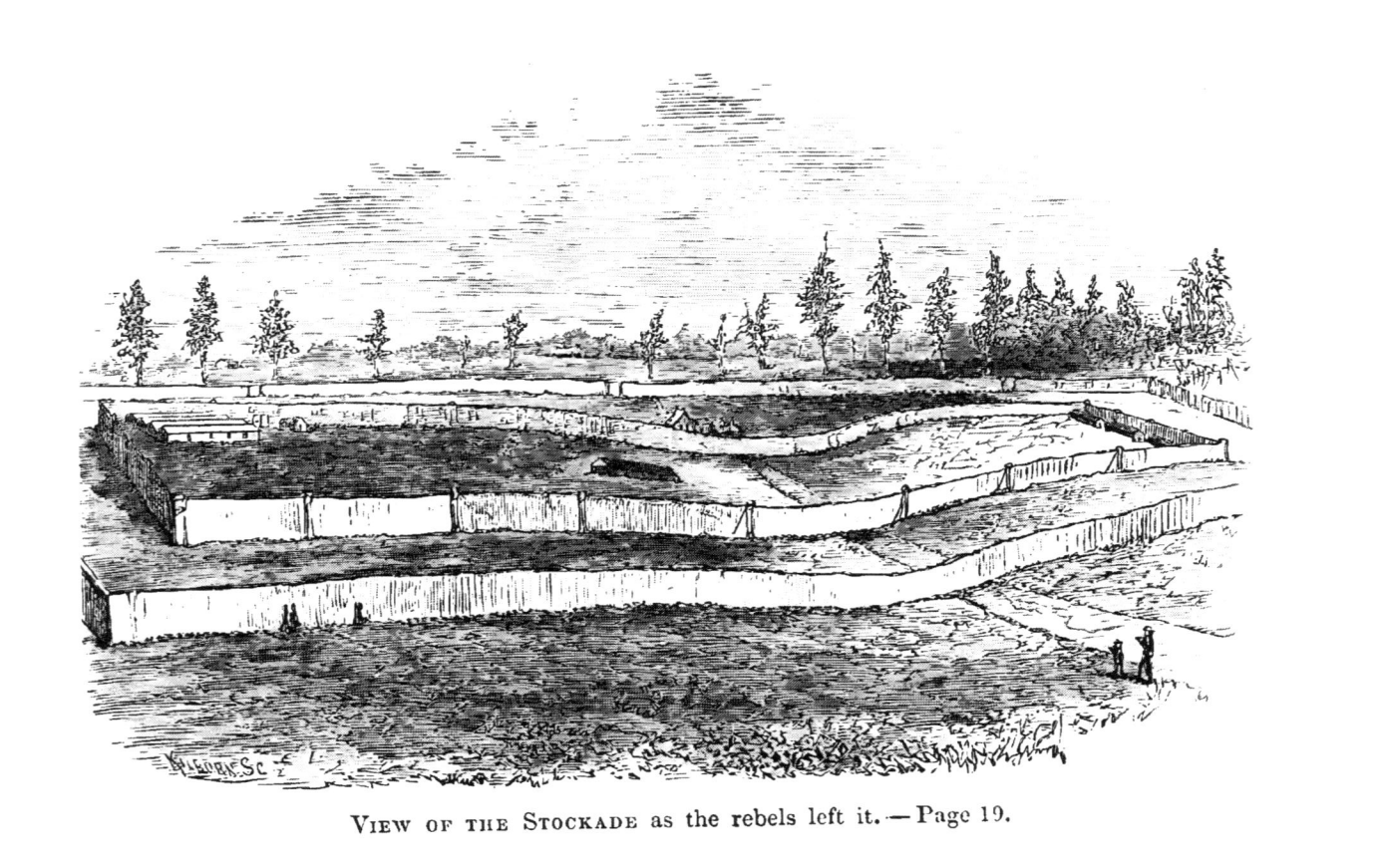

View of the Stockade as the rebels left it. — Page 19.

The surface of the earth was cleared completely as Georgia, as to give full play to the elements of destruction. ...ered

Neither shade nor shelter was there to protect from the storm, or from the merciless rays of an almost tropical sun. Not a tree nor a shrub was left there to cast a shadow over the arid and calcined earth. There was simply a rampart of logs, rising from fifteen to eighteen feet in height above the surface of the ground. This rampart measured at first ten hundred and ten feet in length by seven hundred and seventy-nine feet in width, and was surrounded, at a distance of sixty paces, by another palisade of rough logs more than twelve feet in height. It was afterwards lengthened, in the autumn of 1864, to sixteen hundred and twenty feet.

This enormous structure still stands there, with its giant walls of trees, undisturbed.

<blockquote>
*   *   *   " May none those marks efface,
For they appeal from tyranny to God."
</blockquote>

XII.

A small stream of water, which arose in two branches scarcely a thousand paces distant, in bogs and fens whose bitterness and impurities continued with the current, passed through the central portion of the enclosed space with sufficient volume to supply the wants of many thousand men, if it had been properly received, protected, and economized.

During the summer many springs burst forth from the soil on either bank of the stream within the prison; but

..er, neglected by the military guards, soon became ..ied by the feet and grime of the prisoners, and then this portion of the enclosure, embracing several acres, was transformed into a deep and horrible mire, quivering with those disgusting forms of organic life which are produced by putrid and decaying matter. The stench would have corroded the surface of adamant.

Within the two lines of palisades, and on the western side, was erected the single bakery which was to furnish the munition bread for the prisoners. Upon the hill to the northward, at the distance of two hundred paces from the outer line, was strangely placed the building which was known as the *kitchen*. The reason why this cookery was placed so far from water, and the direct line of communication with the main gate, the projectors alone can tell. Consider the enormous weight of provisions and water which full rations to even ten thousand men would require daily. Consider, then, the distance from the railway depot, the circuitous route to the entrance of the prison, the mode, and inefficient transportation, and you will have an idea of the ignorance, the carelessness, the perversity or wilfulness, or call it what you will, which prevailed here in the prison system, if system it can be termed

XIII.

To the south, on the high land which overlooked the prison and its appendages, was erected the two-story building which served as quarters and offices for the officers and clerks. Along the same elevated ridge were located the well-built huts of the guards, who were selected from the Confederate Reserves of Georgia, under the command of Howell Cobb, and numbered from three to five thousand men. Farther to the west, along the same airy and commanding ridge, and close to the track of the railway, appears the large two-story wooden buildings, which were built and arranged, carefully and comfortably, for the sick of the rebel guards.

XIV.

To the south-east, and at the distance of a stone's throw from the prison, were placed the few miserable and decayed tents which were to serve as hospitals, in mockery of science and humanity.

To-day the traces of this useless philanthropy have passed away, but the results are fearfully shown in the field to the northward, where thirteen thousand soldiers sleep in death, — the harvest of one short year! "Here," said one of the surgeons to the inquirer, "death might be predicted with almost absolute certainty."

Here came a medical officer of the highest rank in the Rebel army, and one of the most eminent *savans* the South, to study the physiology and philosophy of starvation. The notes of that fearful clinic are preserved, and may some future day startle the scientific world with their clearness, their candor, their positive evidence of the cause of death. Thus the scalpel silences the argument, the reasoning of sophistry.

That there was scarcity of medicines, and all of those delicacies known to the cultivated or luxurious taste, there can be no doubt. Neither the country, nor the desires of the people, produced or favored their pio-duction; but let us thank Heaven there is proof that there were some among the medical officers in whom the virtues of the heart were not entirely reversed, who did protest against the needless deficiencies and the system of treatment.

The sufferings here were less poignant than in the pen; for nature always comes to the relief of dying mortals, and tempers the pangs of dissolution.

Food was demanded, but it was wanting. Shelter and the pure air of heaven were prayed for by gasping men; even these, too, were wanting. Yet close by rose the gigantic pines, of the growth of centuries, standing in all the grandeur of the primeval forests, and offering to the disordered vision and senses of the dying wretches grateful shades, cool bowers, or the images of home, and the forms of the well-loved, as the faint and sinking traveller beholds them in the far-off mirage of the desert.

XV.

The dense pine forests on either side still attest the luxuriant growth, which was regarded at the time of its selection as the finest timbered land of all Georgia. These immense pines are even yet so near as to cast their lengthened shadows, at morning and evening, over the accursed area where so many noble men perished for want of shelter from the heat of the noonday sun, the chilling dews of evening, and the frequent rain. The shade temperature of this place sometimes rose to the height of 105°, even 110° Fahrenheit. The sun

VIEW OF OFFICERS' STOCKADE, with rebel camps and hospitals in the distance. — Page 21.

temperature within the stockade must have risen to 120°
and upwards, for the height of the walls prevented the
free circulation of the air. The heat of this region
during the days of summer is unusually great.

Its elevation above the tide level is only about three
hundred feet ; and the hot blasts from the burning
surface of the Gulf of Mexico, which is only about one
hundred and fifty miles distant, sweep up over it northward, without being deviated or modified by ranges of
mountains. The intervening country is unbroken, from
distance to distance, by the undulation of the soil, and
resembles more the level of a wide, green sea than the
usual configurations of the solid earth. It bears the
reputation of being unhealthy, and it is not strange ; for
there are certain isolated local climates which are absolutely pestilential, as we observe in the detached mountain
groups and table lands of India and Southern Europe.
Its isothermal line passes through Tunis and Algiers, and
the hyetal charts show it to be one of the most humid
regions in America.

Fifty-five inches of rain fall here annually, whilst
Maine, with her constant fogs, receives but forty-two
and England but thirty-two.

Was it possible for human life to endure these extremes of heat, rendered still more positive by exposure
to the damp and chilly dews of the nights of southern
latitude? It is a well-known fact, that neither men nor
animals can labor or expose themselves with impunity
to the rays of the noonday sun of tropical climes. Man,
of all terrestrial animals, is the least supplied with natural protectives.

XVI.

Around this ill-fated spot were stretched a cordon of connected earthworks, which completely enveloped the palisades, and commanded, with seventeen guns, every nook and corner of the enclosure. The forts were well constructed, and provided against the chances of sudden and desperate assaults. The cannon were well mounted, and placed in barbette and embrasure. Lunettes and redoubts covered all the approaches to the two great gates.

Several regiments of the rebel reserves constantly occupied the forts and trenches, and guarded closely every avenue. Escape was impossible.

XVII.

To preside over this assemblage, with its arranged, premeditated, and atrocious system, were selected men well known for their energy of purpose and their ferocity of soul, and who hoped, like the Parthian, that cruelty might seem to the eye of man a warlike spirit. Winder has already been summoned to his God, without affording to the tribunals of men the opportunity to judge of his justification or his shame. The wretched Wirz, arraigned and convicted by the most overwhelming evidence, has since paid the severest penalty which the majesty of violated law can exact on earth.

The instincts of nature always demand a certain respect for the memory of the dead, no matter how the death may take place. But shall this shield for the executione' obstruct justice, or reverence and admiration for the remembrance of the virtues of the nobler victims? Let us bring to light, and praise the heroism of noble men, even if we violate and break to pieces the sacred mausoleums where a thousand criminals lie buried.

XVIII.

The dispositions of man depend greatly upon the associations of his early life. The youthful and pliant organization is easily impressed by the natural scenes of birthplace and childhood, and the effect of the views of the savage mountain gorges, the dark and gloomy forests, or the distant landscape, smiling in the rays of the sun, and decorated with the most beautiful works of human industry, are felt hereafter in the labors and conceptions of manhood. Men sometimes are but the living reflections of the savage scenes among which they have been reared, and seldom do we see them arise from that immense and world-wide mass of fallen humanity to cherish anew, to maintain the noble principles of this earthly life, and lead the willing world to the true worship of the Creator.

Wirz was born among the glorious mountains of Switzerland, where the lofty and dazzling peaks of eternal snow, pointing upwards into the clear vault of heaven, impress the human mind with sublimity, or where the deeper glens sadden the heart and blast the aspiring imagination.

It seems that the natural impressions made upon this man in this beautiful country were of an earthly and sor-

did character, for he has always exhibited, in his wander-
ings in pursuit of fortune, the reckless and degraded soul
of a mercenary.

Seeking gain in the New World, he turned up in the
Slave States when the revolt was determined upon, and
without reluctance, offered his services to the frantic and
savage horde. Although a Swiss and republican by
birth and inheritance, he does not hesitate between liberty
and despotism. The principles of political dogmas do
not agitate him; it is the desire for money, and an in-
satiate thirst for blood, blasting the natural heart with
cruel and remorseless passions, that led him blindly and
swiftly to ruin. The fatal plunge taken, and there was
no return. The compunctions of humanity passed over
his seared and unfeeling conscience, with no more effect
than when the waves surge over the huge rocks which
form the bed of the deepest ocean.

He was selected for the fatal position by the brutal
Winder, who first observed him among the unfortunate
prisoners of the first disastrous battle of the republic.
What should recommend him, then, to the notice of
this inhuman officer, can be easily conjectured by the survivors of the prisons of that period. Cruelty then was
pastime, it afterwards became a law. It was then that
some of the chivalry, after the manner of the tribes of
Abyssinia and Eastern Africa, made glorious trophies of
the skulls and the bones of their antagonists who had
fallen in battle.

This man appeared at times kind and humane, and
his voice had the accents of benevolence; but when excited, natural sentiments recoiled with horror at the

depth and extent of his imprecations. This assumed gentleness of disposition is of but little weight among the examples of history.

"I have often said," writes Montaigne, "that cowardice is the mother of cruelty, and by experience have observed that the spite and asperity of malicious and inhuman courage are accompanied with the mantle of feminine softness." The ensanguined Sylla wept over the recital of the miseries he himself had caused.

That daily murderer, the tyrant of Pheres, forbade the play of tragedy, lest the citizens should weep over the misfortunes of Hecuba and Andromache.

The beautiful eyes of the Roman maidens glistened with tears at the imaginary sufferings of the inanimate marbles of Niobe and Laocoon, yet how remorselessly they gave the signal of death to the defeated gladiator on the arena of the Colosseum!

The warm, generous, natural impulses of the heart soon become affected, impaired, and even reversed by brutal associations.

Circumstances develop greatly the characters of men, and they sometimes rise to true greatness, or sink into baseness, according to the law of effect, of contact, and example.

BOOK SECOND.

I.

"Plus in carcere spiritus acquirit, quam caro amittit."

Tertullian.

" Eternal spirit of the chainless mind !
Brightest in dungeons, Liberty ! thou art,
For there thy habitation is the heart —
The heart which love of thee alone can bind :
And when thy sons to fetters·are consigned —
To fetters, and the damp vault's dayless gloom,
Their country conquers with their martyrdom,
And Freedom's fame finds wings on every wind."

Prisoner of Chillon.

WITHIN the deadly shadows of this enormous palisade were assembled and confined together at one time during the hot months of 1864, more than thirty-five thousand soldiers, of the various armies of the United States — more men than Alexander led across the Hellespont to the conquest of Asia ; more men than followed Napoleon in those glorious campaigns over the bright fields of Northern Italy, where every helmet caught some beam of glory.

Here were men of all conditions, birth, and fortune — some of the best blood and sap of the republic.

The strong-limbed lumbermen from the forests of Maine, the tall, gigantic men from the mountains of

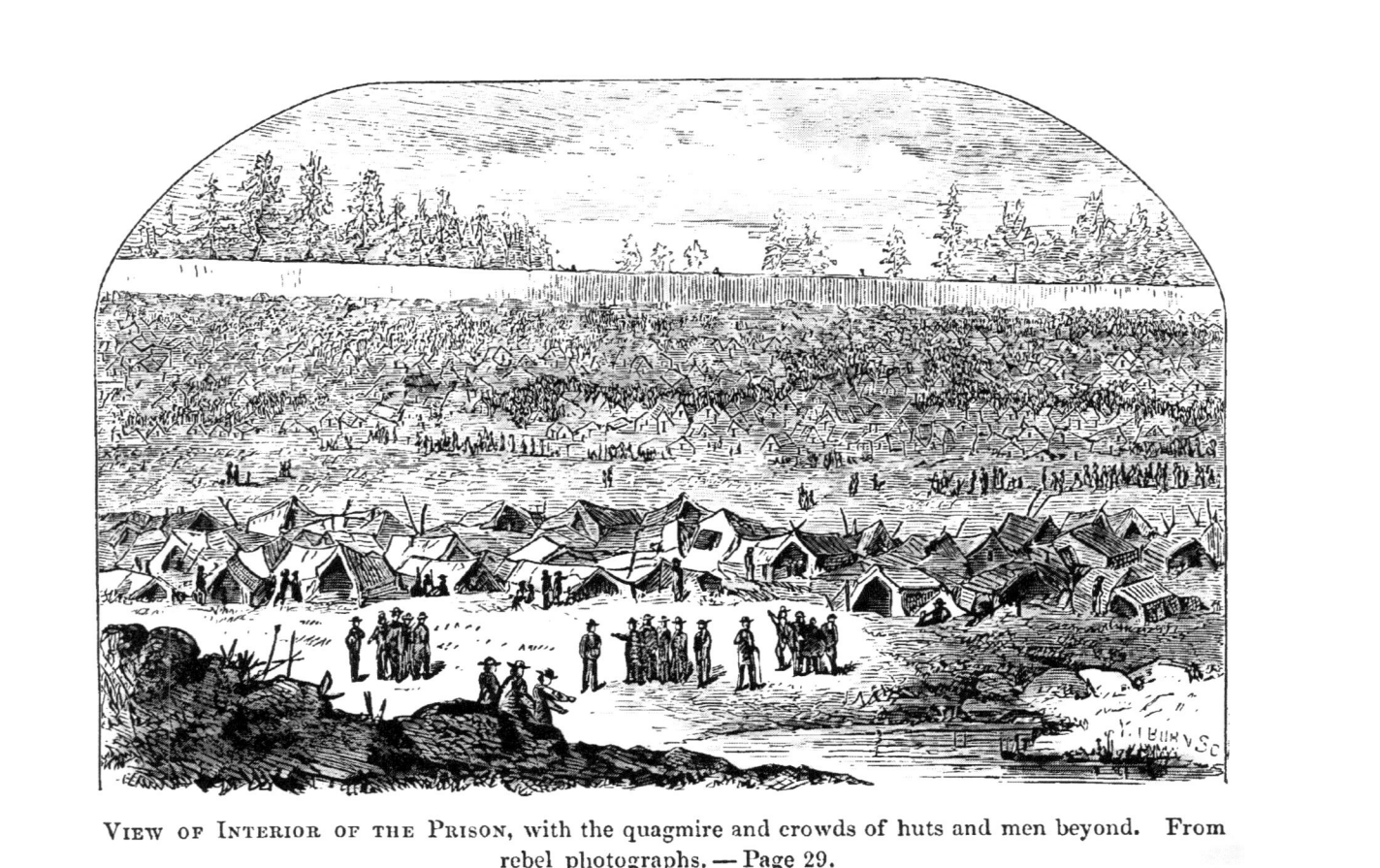

VIEW OF INTERIOR OF THE PRISON, with the quagmire and crowds of huts and men beyond. From rebel photographs. — Page 29.

Pennsylvania, the hunters of the great prairies of the West, — those men of wonderful courage and endurance, — the artisan from the workshop, the student from his books, the lawyer from the forum, the minister from the pulpit, the child of wealth, and the poor widow's only son, were collected here in this field of torture.

They were men in the prime of life — young, vigorous, and active — when they surrendered themselves as prisoners of war. And as prisoners, they were entitled to the care and treatment acknowledged by the general laws and usages of civilized nations, and expected even more from those who boasted of having revived the generosity and chivalric tone of the feudal ages. Besides justice to all men, we owe special grace and benignity to those who come into our power from the hazard of battle. However degraded the suppliant may be, there is always some commerce between them and us, some bond of mutual relation.

Why these men did not receive that respect which true courage always accords to the vanquished brave, why they did not receive even that atom of compassion which belongs to the nature of man, and which is seen even among the lower animals, history, which loves to avenge the weak and oppressed, and which affords to all men, to all nations, the opportunity for their justification, their vengeance, their glory, will surely exhibit in burning characters of horror and shame. There are men even now who would sanctify the acts of cruelty of the rebellion over the very ashes of this the nation's sepulchre. There are men even now who would outrage virtue, and deify the crime. There are men living, like those of the past, but not forgotten iron age, possessed of that remorseless fury, that implacable hatred, which nothing could arrest, nothing could disarm, and which could no more receive a sentiment of compassion than that sophistry which allowed outrage and death to the tender and guiltless child of Sejanus.

"Ut homo hominem, non iratus, non timens, tantum spectaturus occidat."

II.

The intention which directed the formation of this vast camp was Cruelty. The system which governed, or rather the want of system which neglected, each department, whether hospital or commissariat, meant Death. The evidence against the leaders of the Confederacy is not wanting, neither is it obscure. It is true that most of the witnesses have perished, or are fast passing prematurely away; but the chain of circumstantial evidence is so connected, so apparent, that, unless the faith of humanity changes, that voice, which Tacitus calls " the conscience of the human race,'† will, until the end of time, overwhelm with withering scorn the memory of these men as the assassins of sedition, rather than the heroes and saints of a just revolution.

We may search history in vain for a parallel in modern times. Civilization, in its known vicissitudes, cannot point out a spectacle so horrible.

The massacre, in hot blood, of the Tartars of the Crimea by Potemkin, will not compare with this slow, merciless, implacable process of murder by starvation, and violation of those hygienic laws upon which the principle of life depends. The fusilades of that saturnalia of blood, the French Revolution, which swept away whole generations, had the pomp of military executions, which threw a gleam of brilliancy over the scene, and gave momentary enthusiasm to the victims. Those great immolations of the Saracens and Persians by the Tartars were as rapid as the cimeters could flash. "The fury of ideas," says Lamartine, "is more implacable than the fury of men; for men have heart, and opinion none. Systems are brutal forces, which bewail not even that which they crush."

"See," said Timour to the learned men of Aleppo, "I am but half a man, and yet I have conquered Irak, Persia, and the Indies." "Render glory, therefore, to God," replied the Mufti of Aleppo, "and slay no one." "God is my witness," said, with apparent sincerity, the destroyer of so many millions of men, "that I put no one to death by a premeditated will; no, I swear to you I kill no one from cruelty, but it is you who assassinate your own souls."

III.

The world has never seen such a display of courage and devotion as was exhibited by the intelligent masses of the freemen of the North, when the liberties of the great republic were menaced by the fierce gestures of the slave faction and their misguided supporters.

Men of all classes, forsaking home, kindred, and property, rushed to present a living barrier to the impetuous march of the enraged and misguided horde that pressed on with almost resistless fury, and threatened to overwhelm and destroy the noblest fabric of the enlightened mind. At last the carnage of battle has ceased. Nature smiles again, and rapidly obliterates the marks of the ravages left upon her green fields, where the huge and desperate armies have swayed and struggled in deadly conflict. The emblems of civil liberty are again restored, the fasces replaced; and it now becomes the country to arouse itself from the depths of apathy, and revive those sentiments of tenderness and gratitude which nature everywhere bestows upon the memory of those who upheld the cause of liberty, and fell in its defence.

IV.

To understand fully the determined character, the steadfast loyalty, of these brave and unfortunate men, we must consider at length the details of this enclosure, with its hungry, emaciate, filthy mass of humanity, whence arose a stench of death so powerful as to be perceived at the distance of a league — the burning sky, the array of instruments of torture, the manifest design of cruelty.

The suffering wretch had only to pronounce the magic words, "Allegiance to the Rebel cause," and his sufferings and misery were at an end. The huge gates flew open, and with grim smiles, the enfeebled and tottering apostate was welcomed as an accession to the southern ranks.

But the republic was safe here, and the sacred fire of its altars burned steadily through all the horrors and noxious vapors of this hell on earth.

Strange to relate, that out of the seventeen thousand registered sick, there is record of only about *twenty-five* who accepted the offers to save their lives, and took the oath of the rebels. Is it not wonderful that this great number of men should thus, in silence, brave the horrors by which they were surrounded, and remain firm in their convictions of right and wrong? An entire army perished, rather than deny the country which gave them birth! They would no more surrender their principles, than their homes and altars, as ransoms for their lives.

Has the world's history a parallel to this devotion?

> "But these are deeds which should not pass away,
> And names that must not wither, though the earth
> Forgets her empires with a just decay."

V.

Heroism in the damp and noxious prisons, where the noble qualities of the mind are shaken and swayed by the sufferings of the body, is far different from that which is displayed upon the battle-field, amid the glittering and inspiring pomp of war.

The men at Thermopylæ fought in the shadows of the soul-inspiring mountains, and beheld, through the charm of distance, their homes and the beautiful valleys they had sworn to defend. The Decii saw the shining swords of their enemies when they rushed into battle, and the dying nobly and the glory made all fear of death but of little weight.

Here, instead of bright and glorious banners and the flash of arms, the long array of men eager for the con-

2*

test, and the songs, the shouts of defiance, there was a vast ditch, crowded with living beings of scarce the human form, haggard and unnatural in appearance — a sea of red and fetid mud, trampled and defiled by the immense throng. Instead of the white tents and canopies of military encampments, there were the ragged blankets vainly stretched over upright sticks; there were the holes in the earth, the burrows in the sand, like the villages of the rats of the great prairies of the West. They were more like the dens of the beasts of the desert than habitations for human beings.

No Christian hand ever penetrated to their depths to aid the sick and suffering inmates, to nourish the hungry and console the dying, save one Romish priest; and in spite of the horrors and dangers of the place, he was faithful to his trust. Noble man! you have proved by these acts that humanity is not a mendacious idol, and that devotion to humanity is not a mere matter of gain and self-aggrandizement.

More than four thousand human beings perished in these excavations!

It seemed as though vengeance was prolonged beyond death itself.

> " Where was thine Ægis, Pallas, that appalled
> Stern Alaric and Havoc on their way? "

VI.

Life here was brief. The victims, as they entered the gate, were appalled at the horrors that were presented to them in this living sepulchre. Nature seemed to have abandoned the struggle early, and the young men passed, with rapid pace, from youth — that youth so rich in its future — to manhood, from manhood to old age. Neither prudence nor philosophy could protect them from the grievous influences of the morbid conditions to which they were exposed. The delicate and noble faculties were blunted and destroyed. Some perished at once, almost as quickly as though struck by the lightning of heaven, whilst others lingered, according to the strength of the hidden resources, the reserved and superabundant powers of youth.

Among the few survivors of the present day we can learn of the fearful struggle between life and death, by the gray hairs, the impassive features, from which the smile of youth has fled forever, the feeble and tottering steps of the man who has prematurely arrived at his limit of earthly existence.

The integrity and character exhibited by these men, in the midst of these tortures, is unsurpassed.

It was the same morale that immortalized the armies of Italy and Moreau, that covered with splendor the heroes of Sparta and Rome, and proved incontestably the superiority of the volunteer over the mercenary regular. The wretched men died in silence, or with the name of home or the loved ones on their lips, and adjuring their comrades to stand firm in defence of their faith, their country, their God. "My treatment here is killing me, mother; but I die cheerfully for my country." They died as the wounded French died at Jemappes, with the delirium and exaltation of patriotism, uttering at the last moment some of the strains of the songs of freedom, and the names of country and liberty. " Thus the enthusiasm of the combat prolonged or reproduced itself, and survived even in their agony."

The sufferings of these men, wasting, putrefying, dying daily by scores, by hundreds, without touching the remorseless hearts of the prison-keepers, recall to mind those monsters which history points out as rising now and then from out the wreck of social order. It was one of the results of Slavery, for Slavery weakens the natural horror of blood.

Cruelty is naturally progressive, for it engenders the fear of a just revenge. New cruelties succeed, until extermination becomes the rule and ends the scene.

" To hate whom we have injured is a propensity of the human mind," says Tacitus.

VII.

At the distance of about five hundred paces northwestward from the stockade, in a little field which is almost overshadowed by the surrounding pines, appear a multitude of stakes standing upright in the earth, in long and regular lines.

Upon every one of these fragments of boards figures have been carelessly scratched by an iron instrument; and they run up to the appalling number of almost thirteen thousand! Each stick represents a dead man, — a hero, — and this multitude of branchless and leafless trunks reminds us rather of a blasted vineyard than of a cemetery arranged for the human dead.

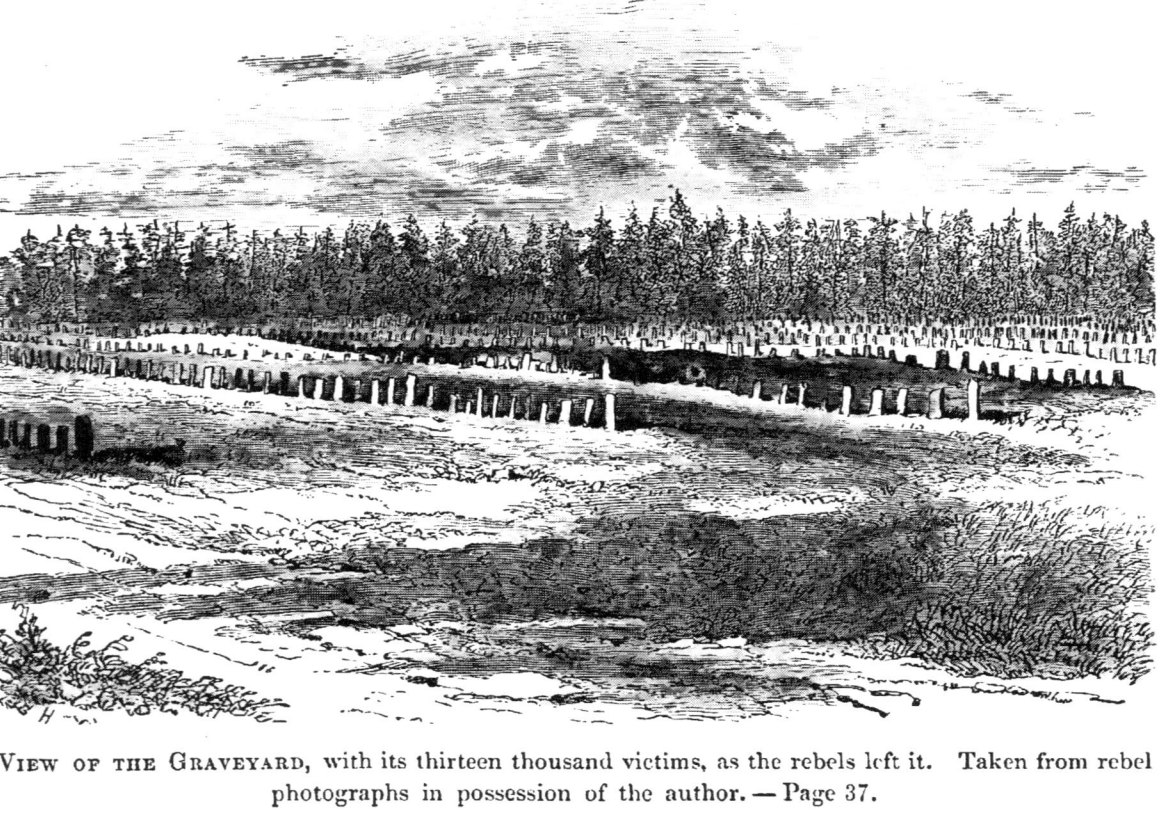

VIEW OF THE GRAVEYARD, with its thirteen thousand victims, as the rebels left it. Taken from rebel photographs in possession of the author. — Page 37.

I have seen many of the rarest sculptures in civilized lands, where art has lavished and exhausted its powers to awaken sympathy for the dead, but have met with none that moved my heart more impressively than the brief, vague inscriptions, the rude memorials of this silent and neglected field, where sleep an entire army of freemen, who preferred lingering death rather than allegiance to a rebel and wicked faction.

Beneath the red clods of this field, thickly as the leaves of autumn, are stretched side by side a number of men more numerous than all of the American soldiers who perished by disease and casualty of battle during the Mexican war — more than all of the British soldiers who were killed, or perished from their wounds, on the bloody fields of the Crimea, the desperate struggles at Waterloo, the four great battles in Spain,—Talavera, Salamanca, Albuera, Vittoria,— and also the sanguinary contest at New Orleans. All these losses of the sons of the British empire do not build up a hecatomb of the human dead so high, so vast, so red, as this one single link of the great chain of wrong that stretched from Virginia to Texas.

There is no battle-field on the face of the globe, known to the antiquary, where so many soldiers are interred in one group as are gathered together in the broad trenches of this neglected field among the pine forests of Georgia. What a gathering is this! What a monument of the incarnation of political lust, of the reckless desperation, the implacability of the depraved human heart, when resolved upon cruelty! The world does not offer, among all of her extant memorials, a more terrible, a more impressive comment upon the ambition, the power, the glory of mankind.

VIII.

Respect to the dead is an instinct of nature; and to leave the remains of a fallen comrade upon the field, unhonored, is repugnant even to the red men of the forest. How much more, then, does a civilized nation, of high degree, owe to the memory of its brave defenders! Will it now forget the noble sacrifice of its sons amid the debasing influences of commerce and manufacture? Shall these sticks, which mark the nation's sacrifice, moulder into dust, and with their brief inscriptions be swept away by the winds of the world, and all traces of this heroism, this martyrdom, lost?

Here is something required more than brief, hollow, human gratitude, and a sonorous, perishable epitaph.

Whatever rises above the level of this plain to commemorate for future ages the devotion of the men who sleep beneath, should be of lasting material, and as colossal as the gigantic proportions of the republic itself: or the field should be levelled and swept, and every distinguishing sign blended and effaced, and the true altar of memorial erected in the hearts of all men who believe and revere those eternal principles of love, justice, truth.

Liberty has but one inscription to offer, and that is the noble lines which were traced on the dungeon wall in the blood of the noblest and purest of the Girondins: "*Potius mori quam fœdari*" — Death rather than dishonor.

IX.

Impartial

a place among th

The law of parole ·sufficient to prevent their
return to service, and their absence from the fields of
campaign would have been of no material weight with
the prolific North.

But the intent of their captors was cruelty; and they
strove to reduce the numbers, and to intimidate the courage, of the Federal soldiers, by acts of savage barbarity,
as the relentless Tartar hoped to terrify the Hindoos into
the profession of Mohammedanism by sacrificing multitudes, and deluging whole countries in blood.

To deny the criminality is, as Lamartine says of the
massacres of September, " to belie the right of feeling of
the human race. It is to deny nature, which is the morality of instinct. There is nothing in mankind greater
than humanity. It is not more permissible for a government than for a man to commit murder. If a drop of
blood stains the hand of a murderer, oceans of gore do
not make innocent the Dantons. The magnitude of the
crime does not transform it into virtue. Pyramids of
dead bodies rise high, it is true, but not so high as the
execration of mankind."

BOOK THIRD.

I.

LET us now examine and consider, with impartial eye, the Stockade in detail — the locality, the hospital, the dietary, and, in fact, all that relates to the condition of life in this region; reviewing at length the laws which regulate the animal economy, and judging of cause and effect with that spirit which Bacon calls the "*prudens quæstio.*"

In selecting new grounds for the habitations of human families, whether in large or limited numbers, particular care must always be observed, especially in warm climes, or where malarial influences are known to prevail. In the selection of places for the encampment of troops, the problem is still more difficult to treat, on account of the general dyscrasial condition of the soldier; and oftentimes far more skill and prudence are required than in the choosing of a field for battle.

How many a noble regiment have we seen impaired in its effective strength, and robbed of its glorious future, by the injudicious encampment, where vain and ignorant officers have sacrificed the health and morale of their men to please their fanciful ideas as to military etiquette — the form of shelter, the position, and the regularity of the prescribed lines of encampment!

(40)

In one of the last campaigns of Europe, when all the resources which modern wealth could afford were lavished with unsparing hand, there was a useless and preventible loss of life, that recalled the most disastrous epidemics of the sixteenth and seventeenth centuries.

War is one of the natural laws for the demolition of the human race, and we see the spirit of destruction silently at work among friends as well as foes. The supreme commands seem mysteriously to be placed in the hands of men who can cause the greatest devastation and sacrifice of life; who march their columns steadily to the deadly and murderous assault when there is no occasion for it; who encamp their troops in pestilential lowlands, when the healthy heights offer safer and better accommodations.

"Nobilitas cum plebe perit, lateque vagatur ensis."

II.

It is a melancholy fact, attested by the distinguished Marshal Saxe, that the military men of modern times are far less informed than the great generals of antiquity in the profound knowledge of public hygiene, and especially of that which relates to the economy of armies. We can admire, but hardly improve, the physical education imposed upon the volunteers of Sparta and the legionaries of Rome; and we have not surpassed their scientific, yet rude alimentation, by which they marched over immense distances with rapidity, and preserved their vigor and morale. From the extant documents of the ancients, from Xenophon or Vegetius, it is shown that their acquaintance with whatever related to clothing, encampment, food, the graduation of exercises, and the employ of forces, was of the highest character.

The effects of high and low lands, of good and bad water, on the diseases, energy, character, and intellect of man, have been sketched in a masterly manner by Hippocrates.

The exposure of a few hours to malignant influences may impair the strength of an army to such a degree as to thwart the most skilful plans, the wisest combinations for vigorous campaigns, as, for instance, the Walcheren expedition of the English, the Neapolitan campaign of France. when her army was reduced from twenty-eight thousand to four thousand effective men, in one hundred hours, from an injudicious encampment at Baie, or when Orloff lost his army in Paros, or, still later, the disaster to the splendid division of the French army under Espinasse, in the fatal Dobrutscha.

Armies have been lost, the fate of empires decided, by the violation or neglect of the simple rules of hygiene; and all through the blood-stained pages of military history do we observe examples, from the time when Scipio lost the battle of Trebbia, or when Bajazet threw away his vast empire on the plains of Angora, down to Kunersdorf, when the impetuosity of Frederick the Great would not allow rest to his men or horses.

III.

In 1863 the depots near Richmond became so crowded by the Federal prisoners that it became a matter of serious consideration to the rebel authorities how to guard them, and attempt to feed them and the regiments guarding them. Then the idea was conceived of forming a great camp in the Gulf States, in a locality fruitful in grain, and in a position secure from raids from the Federal cavalry. Several locations were examined, but none pleased the selecting officer, until he had examined the site at Andersonville, to which he conceived a particular fancy. There were places in this section of the country where pure water could be obtained in abundance, but these spots were not so readily accessible, and wood was not so plenty and handy as at this. There was another consideration in the public view of its selection, that it was in the heart of the best corn-producing region at that time in Georgia, and easy access could be had with the everglades of Florida, where herds of half wild cattle roamed at will.

It is not the belief of the writer, although there are many facts to warrant such an inference, that the selection was made with the view of deliberately destroying the prisoners openly, and without reserve, for there were other localities far more pestilential than this ; and yet, on the other hand, there were also many situations infinitely more salubrious and easy of access. There was in reality not much reflection in the matter. The selectors thought only of the geographical and strategical position ; they cared not for its topography or its meteorology.

They consulted only their convenience. The idea of the preservation of the lives of their unfortunate prisoners never troubled their minds, never disturbed their conscience. They would build a safe and secure pen, and if God, in his infinite and mysterious mercy, chose to summon from earth any of the hapless wretches, they would not consider themselves as accountable for the premature deaths. Such was their reasoning. Such was their philosophy. Such was their conscience. The exult of Winder, when asserting that he was doing more for the Confederacy than a dozen regiments at the front, and the exclamation of Howell Cobb, when pointing to the ten thousand graves, " That is the way I would do for them," were perhaps the bravado of the southern slaveholder. Even at this late date we can find men, of some tenderness, in this vicinity, who have reasoned their weak minds into the idea and belief that no harm was ever done or intended ; and even if it can be proved, then the Federals only received what they deserved, and no more than their own sons in the prisons of the North endured.

Such was the conscience of the Pharisee.

Such was the remark made to the writer by a southern gentleman over the graves of the victims.

IV.

The topographical features of the site are not particularly objectionable for an encampment of a few hundred men.

The northern and southern banks incline sufficiently towards the stream in the centre to allow of proper drainage. The stream itself furnished water in sufficient volume to provide for the wants of ten thousand men, if it had been turned from its channel above the stockade, and introduced into the prison by simple sluices. But to this important item there was not the least attention paid.

To preface the analysis of this stockade, &c., we may wisely review the remarks of the late Dr. Jackson, the chief medical officer of the British army.

v.

" A necessity occurs in war, on many occasions, which leaves no option of choice in occupying posts of an unhealthy character : but there is, unfortunately, an authority, derived from example and the sanction of great names, which directs the military officer, when under no military necessity, to fix his encampment on grounds which are unhealthy in themselves, or which are exposed by position to the influence of noxious causes, which are carried from a distance.

" Such advice proceeds from the desire to act on a presumption of knowledge, which cannot be ascertained, rather than to act by the experience of facts, which man is qualified to observe and verify.

" It is consonant with the experience of military people, in all ages and in all countries, that camp diseases most abound near the muddy banks of large rivers, near swamps, and ponds, and on grounds which have been recently stripped of their woods. The fact is precise : but it has been set aside to make way for an opinion.

" It was assumed, about half a century since, by a celebrated army physician, that camp diseases originate from causes of putrefaction, and that putrefaction is connected radically with a stagnant condition of the air. As streams of air usually proceed along rivers, with more certainty and force than in other places, and as there is evidently a more certain movement of air, that is, more winds, on open grounds than among woods and thickets, this sole consideration, without any regard to experience, influenced opinion, and gave currency to the destructive maxim, that the banks of rivers, open grounds, and exposed heights, are the most eligible situations for the encampment of troops. They are the best ventilated: they must, if the theory be true, be the most healthy. The fact is the reverse. But demonstrative as the fact may be, fashion has more influence than multiplied examples of fact, experimentally proved.

" Encampments are still formed in the vicinity of swamps, or on grounds which are newly cleared of their woods, in obedience to theory, and contrary to fact. The savage, who acts by instinct, or who acts directly from the impressions of experience, has in this instance the advantage over the philosopher, who, reasoning concerning causes he cannot know, and acting according to the result of his reasonings, errs and leads others astray by the authority of his name.

" The savage feels, and acting by the impression of what he feels, instead of fixing his habitation on the exposed bank of large rivers, unsheltered heights, or grounds newly cleared of their woods, seeks the cover of the forests, even avoids the streams of air which proceed from rivers, from the surface of ponds, or from lands newly opened to the sun. The rule of the savage is a rule of experience, founded in truth, and applicable to the encampment of troops, even of civilized Europeans.

" In accordance with this principle, it is almost uniformly true, *cæteris paribus*, that diseases are more common, at least more violent, in broken, irregular, and hilly countries, where the temperature is liable to sudden changes, and where blasts descend with fury from the mountains, ⸱ in large and extensive inclined plains, under the .on of equal and gentle breezes only. From this .act, it becomes an object of the first consideration, in choosing ground for encampments, to guard against the impression of strong winds, on their own account, independently of their proceeding from swamps, rivers, and noxious soils.

" In countries covered with woods, abundantly supplied with straw, and other materials applicable to the purpose of forming shelter, it is, upon the whole, better to raise huts and construct bowers than to carry canvas. The individual is exercised by labor, and as his mind is employed in contriving and executing something for self-accommodation, he is furnished with a daily opportunity of renewing the pleasure. The mode of hutting, here recommended, effectually precludes the evils arising from those contaminations of air in which contagion is generated — an evil which often arises in tents, and is carried about with an army in all its movements in the field."

* * * * *

The view of the ancients in regard to the encampment of troops may be understood from the counsel of Vegetius: " Ne aridis et sine opacitate arborum campis, aut collibus ne sine tentoriis æstate milites commorentur."

VI.

As we have remarked before, the site of the prison was covered with trees when its outlines were traced and surveyed by the rebel engineers. These trees, felled to the ground, were hewn, and matched so well on the inner line of the palisades as to give no glimpse of the outer

world across the space of the dead line, which averaged nineteen feet in width, and which was defined by a frail wooden railing about three feet in height, from fifteen to twenty-five feet distant from the palisades.

This line of stockade rose from fifteen to eighteen feet above the surface of the ground, while the outer line of logs, which was erected about sixty paces distant from the inner line, was formed of the rough trunks of pines, and projected twelve feet above the earth. The original stockade measured but ten hundred and ten feet in length, and seven hundred and eighty-three feet in width; and within this space were jammed together, for several months, from twenty-two thousand to thirty-five thousand men, thus giving a superficial area to each man, when the prison contained thirty thousand prisoners, but seventeen square feet, after deducting the nineteen feet average for the dead line, and the quagmire, three hundred feet in width. This measurement would allow for thirty-five thousand men but fifteen square feet of area, or less than two square yards to each person, or more than twenty times the density of Liverpool. This was all the space that was afforded before the enlargement, and this reckoning does not include roads or by-paths for communication among the prisoners.

Seventeen and a half square feet of earth are allowed for the coffin's length in the field of sepulchres. There were here to be seen twelve acres of living men, packed together like the immense shoals of fish in the ocean, but like nothing that has life on the earth, not even the ant-fields. The ratio of density was equivalent to more than sixteen hundred thousand people to the square mile. The densest portion of East London has the great number of one hundred and sixty thousand to the square mile.

VII.

In the month of August the stockade was lengthened six hundred and ten feet, by what influence or from what cause it is unknown ; but nevertheless it was enlarged to the length of sixteen hundred and twenty feet, — thus making the entire area sixteen hundred and twenty by seven hundred and eighty-three feet. This enlargement was a salutary movement on a small scale, but it only prolonged the sufferings of the victims. The thirty thousand men had now twenty-two acres, minus the dead line and marsh, or thirty square feet per man, or three and a half square yards. There were actually, during this month, thirty-five thousand men within the prison, and some authorities give me as high as thirty-six thousand. This density is enormous, and cannot be tolerated by animal life in any climate, in any latitude, of the world. There must be space for organic life to develop and maintain itself, otherwise it perishes. To give a correct idea of the crowded condition of this pen, we do not know where to turn for example. The great cities of civilized lands do not even approximate in their ratio of populations.

The relation of density, in the three great divisions of London, give thirty-five, one hundred and nineteen, and one hundred and eighty square yards to each inhabitant. The densest portion of Liverpool, with its lofty and immense brick ranges of buildings, swarming with industrial life, gives more than eighty square feet to each person. The early Roman camps, which are a marvel to military men, and the closest known to military science, gave to the ordinary legion three hundred and sixty-seven square feet of area to each man. The plans of Polybius give two hundred and thirty square feet to each soldier of the consular army of two legions, numbering nearly eighteen thousand men, and the descriptions of Hyginus give similar ratios.

The encampments of the United States infantry afford, in the most restricted portion (between stacks of arms and kitchens), two hundred and forty-four square feet per man, or seventeen hundred and thirty-one square feet per man for the whole camp.

The space allowed by law for barracks alone is fifty-four square feet for each soldier, reckoned on the basis of a full complement of men. The rules of the rebel army concerning camps are the same as those of the regulations of the United States army.

The United States prison at Elmira contained six thousand men, and extended over forty acres. The other prisons, at Chicago, Johnson's Island, Point Lookout, and Fort Delaware, were provided with spacious exercise grounds, and furnished with covered barracks, built of proper form, and fitted up with the required conveniences of life. Belle Isle, which held ten thousand prisoners, had but six acres, and no shelter, no conveniences whatever.

Andersonville, which contained over thirty thousand prisoners, had in the stockade, before enlargement, but eighteen acres in all, and but twelve acres for the use of the prisoners, minus the dead line and the marsh.

The prison at Dartmoor, in England (which was a paradise in comparison with Andersonville), where our prisoners were held in captivity by the English during the last war, furnished two hundred to three hundred square feet to every prisoner in the barracks, besides allowing spacious yards, where the prisoners were permitted to exercise daily. There were there seven large two-story stone buildings, each one hundred and eighty feet in length. Five thousand prisoners enclosed within twenty acres of land at Dartmoor, thirty thousand in twelve acres, or thirty-five thousand in twenty-two acres, at Andersonville.

VIII.

The timbers composing the stockade were of entire trunks of pines, massive and solid, and measuring from one to three feet in diameter. They were sunk into the earth for about five or six feet, and held in position at the top by long, slender pines, nailed on the outer side by large iron spikes. There were but two gates for this vast prison, and but two corresponding apertures in the outer palisade. These gates were constructed of massive timbers, and protected by a strong porch, occupying a base of about thirty feet square. These were always strongly guarded, to prevent the sudden rush of masses of men. At intervals of about one hundred feet, were erected detached and covered platforms, upon the outer side of the palisades, which, overlooking the summit of the wall, and the enclosure beyond, served as sentry boxes. The sentries, perched buzzard-like on the wall, could observe, from their high positions, at all times, the actions, the motions of the uncovered prisoners, and with their rifles shoot down the offending prisoner, whether he stood

talking with his comrades, in the centre of the space, or whether he approached the sacred precincts of the dead line.

Sometimes they threw down their unconsumed fragments of bread to the hungry men. Sometimes they were hurled with curses; rarely were they thrown from feelings of compassion. Yet there were some kind-hearted men here, in the degrading position of the sentry box, who viewed the scene with affright, and who wept bitterly over the awful torture and sacrifice of life.

The author, travelling on foot among the mountains and forests of Northern Georgia, after peace was declared, found these evidences of humane feeling among the letters preserved in the humble cabins of the poor whites. That unoffending men were shot down without warning, there is no doubt whatever; that men, weary of torture, staggered to the dead line, and calmly, joyfully received the fatal shot, there is positive evidence.

IX.

The trees were all removed from the enclosure, and with the specific intent of cruelty, as was openly stated by the brutal builders. They should have no shade, it was said, and no shade had the wretched men but what was cast by the few ragged and rotten blankets and shelter tents that the prison examiners passed by as utterly worthless in their examination and search for articles of value, whether watches, bank notes, hats, shirts, and even shoes. There were men who, robbed at the outer gates, entered the prison almost naked. This system of robbery was open and audacious, and it is said that the only prisoners who escaped spoliation were those who were taken from Sherman when Atlanta fell, and when consternation prevailed at the prison in consequence. It is positively stated that it was sanctioned by Wirz and Winder. At all events, two men, by the names of Hume and Duncan, robbed the prisoners systematically, and appropriated the packages sent to the prisoners, from the United States, to such an extent that few if any articles ever reached the poor men to whom the boxes of food and clothing were sent.

These blankets and rags were vainly stretched over sticks, to form the semblance of a habitation, wherever the earth gave firm foothold, even along the borders of the pestilential marsh. Those who were destitute of even these shreds of cloth, dug with their hands holes in the

earth, after the example of wild beasts, or with the slimy
water from the brook they built up, with handfuls of mud,
little cabins over hollows scooped out from below the
surface of the ground, and as rude as the clumps of earth,
which that lowest degree of the human form — the Digger
Indian — inhabits.

These may be seen at the present day, looking like the
lodges of the beaver, or the mounds of the marmots of the
prairies, and half concealed by those wild, useless, and
noxious weeds which linger in, and cling to the footsteps
of man, as he wanders in his migrations over the uncultivated lands of the globe.

Sometimes the heavy rains washed away the roofs of
mud, inundating the occupants beneath. Some of the

poor wretches had not the strength to lift up the incumbent mass of earth, and perished miserably in their dens. There are now in these demolished excavations the bones of some of our fellow-citizens, unknown and unhonored. The cry of distress was so constant that few heeded the smothered moan. The stumps of the fallen trees were grubbed up by the knives and fingers of the prisoners for firewood to warm themselves with, or to cook their scanty food; even the roots were followed down deep into the earth, for the purpose of obtaining the means of warmth which were almost entirely denied them by the prison keepers.

X.

There is no excuse for this wanton exposure to the vicissitudes of the climate, for the forests adjoining were immense in their extent, and thousands of the suffering men offered, begged to go and obtain material to build sheds or huts to protect them from the inclemency of the weather. Neither parole was allowed for this purpose, nor real attempts made to obtain the building tools. To show the force of the argument that the rebels had not sufficient aid, and that it would have been dangerous to have paroled any of these prisoners, there is the fact that there were several large steam saw-mills in the vicinity, and they could have easily afforded, in few weeks, all the lumber required for the purpose of shelter.

Was it recklessness, was it perversity, or was it malice aforethought, that withheld from the prisoners the means of shelter? The few sheds that were erected were not commenced until late in the term of its occupa-

VIEW OF THE MANNER IN WHICH THE DEAD WERE INTERRED. The bodies were laid in rows of one hundred to three hundred, and after the earth was thrown over them a stake was thrust down to mark the place of burial. This view is taken from a rebel photograph. — Page 57.

tion, too late to render much service. They were merely roofs of boards, placed upon posts, at the distance of seven feet from the ground. There were neither sides nor partitions to these sheds, and they were not required during the hot months.

Pity was not a virtue that was recognized here: the noble impulses of the heart were reversed, and the natural instincts perverted.

The dead bodies of the thousands who perished within the stockade, without medical attendance, were dragged forth, without care, and thrown promiscuously into the common field-carts, which, with their carelessly heaped-up burdens, proceeded to the trenches, where the dead heroes were laid in long lines, side by side, two or three hundred in a trench, and then a stick was thrust into the ground, at the head of each man, to indicate the place of burial. For the care observed in the burial of the dead after the carts arrived at the cemetery, and the preserving of the records of the victims, and the place, we are indebted to our own men, who were paroled especially for the purpose.

The only solicitude observed by the rebels during or after interment of their victims, was shown by the civil engineer or surveyor of the town. He thought that so much animal matter should not go entirely to waste, and so commenced to plant grape vines over the mounds of the decomposing dead.

To show the utter want of decency which ruled all things connected with the prison, it is stated by positive eye-witnesses that the same carts that transported the dead, went forth (without being cleansed of their reeking

3 *

and disgusting filth), to the shambles and the depots for the meat and corn for the living prisoners.

XI.

An eminent statistician has stated that mortality is in direct ratio to the density of population, and that superficial area is as essential to health as cubic space. To the writer's mind, the overcrowding of the men, and their exposure to the variations of heat and cold, the influence of moisture, and the foul emanations of the infected soil, were sufficient to cause great destruction of human life ; and when combined with the deficient dietary, the imagination can hardly conceive of a better field for disease and death than the condition of this swarming pen. All the elements and combinations of physical destructiveness were here in full play. " Losses by battle," says Sir Charles Napier, " sink to nothing, compared with those inflicted by improperly constructed barracks, and the jamming of soldiers — no other word is sufficiently expressive." " Diseases," states the French Inspector Baudens, " slay more men than steel or powder, and it is often easy to prevent them by a few simple hygienic precautions."

In all campaigns where the care of the soldier is left to the military man, — who is educated for destruction, and has not been taught in the economy of life, — we see in the mortuary and non-efficient lists a disgraceful and culpable array of thoughtless routine, vulgar prejudices, and systems. In our Military Academies the elements and the means of destruction are taught, but not a law unfolded that relates to the principles of health, strength,

nd life. To alleviate the burden of the military list by
anitary measures is an idea unheard of, or at least un-
oticed. "For these works," writes Chadwick, in his
apers on "Economy," "a special training is needed for
ur military engineers, whose present peculiar training is
nly for old works for war, and for those imperfectly, —
orks for the maintenance of the health of an army
eing necessary means to the maintenance of its mili-
iry strength.

"The one-sided character of the common training of
ur military engineers was displayed in the Crimea, in
ie proved need of a sanitary commission to give in-
ruction for the selection and the practical drainage of
roper sites for healthy encampments, for the choice col-
:ction and the proper distribution of wholesome water,
ir the construction of wholesome huts, and the proper
helter and treatment of horses as well as men."

XII.

In this enclosure, during a period of twelve months,
rom five thousand to thirty-six thousand human beings
te, slept, and drank, whilst the piles of filth were con-
tantly accumulating, and the germs of infection silently
t work. There was no regularity in the arrangement of
he interior. Men collected in groups in the day time,
nd they lay in rows, like swine, at night.

The stream, which with little ingenuity could have
ieen turned to a blessing for the prison, was allowed to
ie obstructed by the heaps of grime; and enlarging its
irea, it assisted in forming the extensive quagmires,

which were several acres in extent. So little care was observed for the comfort or the health of the prisoners, that all the washings of the bakery, all the filth of the out-houses of the workmen, were allowed to pass down and mingle with the current of the stream only thirty feet above the point of entrance into the stockade. The traveller can observe to-day that this malicious act of refined cruelty, or fatal error in hygiene, was really perpetrated.

Besides this, the drains of the camp and the town above emptied themselves into this stream which supplied the prison with water.

XIII.

The bakery was located on the west side of the stockade, about equidistant from either line of palisade. It was of rough boards, and but one story in height. Its interior disclosed two rooms, one of which communicated with the two ovens, which were built of common brick. These two ovens — fourteen feet in length by seven feet in width, and with one kneading-trough fifteen feet long, and less than three feet in width — supplied the prisoners with all the bread they obtained; and so far the writer has not learned that there was any other source of supply.

These same ovens, kept red hot, and worked night and day, to the fullest capacity, by the commissary bakers of the United States service, could not have produced but eight thousand rations of white bread, and but nine thousand six hundred rations of corn bread. This is the extreme limit; and regarded by the workmen, who have made the calculations, as almost an impossibility. The ordinary capacity of this establishment was probably about four or five thousand rations of corn bread. This quantity, divided daily among thirty thousand men, would

give but a small morsel to each one; and this gives the appearance of truth to the statement, that from two to six ounces of corn bread were furnished as rations to the prisoners.

Ask a survivor of this prison treatment, if perchance you can find one, how he preserved his life, and he will tell you, "By eating the rations of the dying." Ten thousand men were sick or dying in this enclosure at one time.

After the carts, with their scanty burdens of food, had passed into the prison, and distributed their contents, ten or fifteen thousand of the haggard and starving men might be seen collected together in the central portion of the prison trading with each other. Some of the poor

wretches would be offering a handful of peas for a knot
of wood no larger than the human fist, in order that they
might cook their allowance; others offering, in barter,
their remnants of clothing — a cap, or a shoe, or anything they possessed — for a morsel of food.

abThe little knots of wood above mentioned had a standard value of fifty cents; yet there were immense forests
all around, and within sight on every side.

XIV.

There appears to have been but one kitchen for this
vast assemblage, and that strangely situated — far in rear
of the outer palisade, away from water-course or spring.
The soil to-day does not present traces of a much-trav-
elled road from its doorway to the main gate, distant
about one third of a mile by the route taken. Consider
the enormous weight of provisions which should have
passed over this road when the prison contained more
than twenty thousand men. This kitchen was a plain
one-story shed, built of rough boards, one hundred feet
in length, and less than fifty feet in width. It contained in
the interior two medium-sized ranges, and four boilers of
fifty gallons' capacity each. The capacity indicated does
not by far equal the cooking apparatus which is required
and furnished to the Lincoln and Harewood Hospitals,
of Washington, for twelve hundred men.

It is the opinion of the writer, who is familiar with the
amount of cooking apparatus required by large hospitals
and camps, that this kitchen, with its implements, could

not, in the course of twenty-four hours, by constant relays of industrious workmen, have furnished cooked
rations to more than five thousand men. There may
have been other arrangements for cooking in the open
air; but there are no longer any traces of such opera-
tions, nor has the writer any evidence that such was
the case.

XV.

Upon the banks of the same stream, and near the railroad station, was erected the stockade which was intended for the confinement of the officers; but it was
abandoned, after few weeks' occupation, partly from motives of prudence and in fear of revolt in keeping officers
near so great a number of the rank and file of the army,
and partly from the unfortunate selection of the locality.
The officers were removed to Macon, and were confined
there in the cotton sheds during a long period. This

pen, known as the officers' stockade, was built of pine-tree palisades, fifteen feet high, and measured one hundred and ninety-five feet in length by one hundred and eight feet in width, and was provided with a shed in the interior forty-five feet long by twenty-seven feet wide, and also with a walk, suspended on the outside of the palisade, for the use of the sentries. The location and the provisions of this stockade were worse and more dangerous than even the main prison.

XVI.

On the pathway to the graveyard, not far from the prison, and in open sight, was built the hut where the bloodhounds were kept, always ready to track and pur-

sue the fugitives, who were so fortunate as to escape by
evading the vigilance of the guards, or by the slow and
dangerous process of tunnelling beneath the palisades.
The system of pursuit was so perfect, the dogs so
numerous and well trained, that it was very rarely that
any one escaped, and then it was only by the kind intervention of the black man.

There were but nine bloodhounds kept here, but there
were more than fifty dogs, kept in relays, along the route
of escape, extending from the town to the city of Macon,
fifty miles distant. The names of these inhuman wretches,
who kept and hunted with these hounds, are known to
the writer, the places of their residence, the number of
their animals, and the price they received for each hapless victim overpowered by their dogs. These packs of
hounds were generally accompanied by dogs of fierce
and determined courage, to seize and hold the object pursued until the hunters arrived. The ordinary bloodhound
of these regions is cowardly from degeneration, and dare
not face the look, nor disregard the voice of man, and
until the catch-dogs arrive and dash in, and lead the way,
they bay and show their teeth from safe distances; but
the victim once disabled, they tear and rend the living
limbs without reluctance. The bloodhound is said,
when in a state of tranquillity, to be the most affectionate
of all the canine race, but when once excited, he no
longer recognizes the blood of his master from that of
the stranger. That many men were pursued, and caught,
and paid for by the rebel authorities, at the price of
thirty dollars a head, there is abundant proof; that men
were disabled, and torn wantonly by the hounds, and

afterwards died of their wounds, the writer has positive proof. That Federal soldiers were overpowered and destroyed in the forests by the dogs, and their brutal owners, there is evidence.

It did not shock the civil communities of the South to hear of the use of the bloodhounds to pursue and maim men of their own race and nation, for in every locality, for a long period past, it had been the custom to rear and train dogs to catch the hapless slave who had incurred the rage of his master, and vainly sought to escape from his fury in the obscure recesses of the tangled forests.

Usage, by long repetition, had blunted the natural sympathies, so that hate readily excused the difference in class and color.

XVII.

The bloodhounds here used appear to have been of a degenerate breed, and to have lacked the great strength, the invincible determination, which the true race possesses. The bloodhounds introduced into Cuba, to exterminate the Indians, were ferocious and powerful animals. From these the present stock in Southern Georgia were probably descended, and during three centuries of change, have gradually lost their nobler qualities, but have preserved the form. The true bloodhound is taller than the fox-hound, and stronger in his make. His color is of a reddish brown, shaded here and there with darker tints. His muzzle and jaws wide and strong, and the frame firmly knit. His scenting power is extraordinary, and from time immemorial his services have been made use of in tracking wounded animals or fugitives from justice.

> " Soon the sagacious brute, his curling tail
> Flourished in air, low bending, plies around
> His busy nose, the steaming vapor snuffs
> Inquisitive, nor leaves one turf untried,
> Till, conscious of the recent stains, his heart
> Beats quick; his snuffing nose, his active tail
> Attest his joy : then with deep, opening mouth,
> That makes the welkin tremble, he proclaims
> Th' audacious felon : foot by foot he marks
> His winding way, while all the listening crowd
> Applaud his reasonings, o'er the watery ford,
> Dry sandy heaths, and stony, barren hills ;
> O'er beaten paths, with men and beasts disdained,
> Unerring he pursues, till at the cot
> Arrived, and seizing by his guilty throat
> The caitiff vile, redeems the captive prey."

BOOK FOURTH.

I.

ANIMALS eat that they may live. Man eats, not only that he may live, but that he may gather strength, and fulfil his high destiny on earth.

When God gave form and animation to the dust of the earth, and man appeared, he did not intend that the sustenance of life should be left to chance or to careless selection. This intent of the Creator is revealed in the study of the organic world, where wonderful varieties and productions are offered to the appetite of man, in order that the "force of the universe may glow within his veins," and that the faculties of his mind may so expand that he may behold and comprehend the works and designs of his Maker.

Food, next to the purity of the air, determines the degree of the physical well-being; it gives the beauty of contour to the form ; it builds up the marvellous structure of the brain ; the ravishing smile of the features, the sublimity of thought, depend alike in great measure upon the benign influence of food.

It not only gives to nations their characteristics of strength and solidity, but it bestows upon society more of grace and refinement than philosophy is willing to allow.

II.

The question of alimentation with the civil laborer, exposed to healthy influences of properly distributed air and sunlight, and to the regular motions of a well-conducted life, is easy of solution to the inquiring mind.

But when it relates to the soldier, subjected to strange and unhealthy influences, the explanations involve much study, care, and research.

In the natural condition of man it is easy to determine how much food will support life and sustain physical exertion. The dietaries of the public institutions of different countries, the experiments of physiologists, and the records of history give the data with sufficient clearness. As to the amount of food required daily to repair the waste and wants of the human organism, much depends upon the degree of muscular exertion and nervous excitation, as well as the temperature of the season. In the alimentation of armies scientific principles must not be disregarded. Food must be considered as force; it must contain, not only material, but power. The strength of men, says Baron Liebig, is in direct ratio to the plastic matter in their food.

In determining the absolute quantities of nutrient substances required by the system, Lehman observes that there are three magnitudes especially to be considered.

The first is the quantity requisite to prevent the animal from sinking by starvation. The second is that which affords the right supply of nourishment for the perfect accomplishment of the functions, and the last is that which indicates the amount of nutrient matter which may, under the most favorable circumstances, be subjected to metamorphosis in the blood. No one of the four classes, the carbohydrates, the fats, the albuminous matters, and the salts, will answer the purpose alone, but all must be employed together, and this invariable proportion according to the local, and, therefore, variable waste of the system. These considerations indicate how complicated the problem is.

III.

Life is an action; the principle of life, whatever may be its nature, is eminently and visibly a principle of excitation, of impulsion, a motive power.

" It is taking a false idea of life," says Cuvier, " to consider it as a simple link which binds the elements of the living body together, since, on the contrary, it is a power which moves and sustains them unceasingly."

These elements do not for an instant preserve the same relation and connection; or, in other words, the living body does not for an instant keep the same state and composition. " This law," adds Flourens, " does not affect alone the muscles, viscera, and tissues, but there is a continual mutation of all the parts composing the bone." These views have been substantiated by the extended experiments of Chossat, of Von Bibra, and a host of experimentalists, showing how positive and decided are the changes in the material composition of the body, and especially the constitution of even the bone from the influence of food.

IV.

" It is from the blood that life derives the principles which maintain and repair it. The more vigorous, plastic, and rich in nutritive material, so much the more life increases and manifests itself, so much the quicker the reparatory processes restore a lesion to its natural condition.

" The blood owes its vivifying properties to the presence of oxygen, which it receives by the respiratory organs; but that nourishing fluid, to complete its physiological *rôle*, needs to receive combustible and organizable material."

These Protean principles of the healthy blood form one fifth of its weight.

Oxygen unites with the carbon of the food in the blood of animals; carbonic acid is formed and heat evolved. When the atmosphere is vitiated, the oxygenating processes are diminished in ratio to the vitiation.

The experiments of Seguin, Crawford, and De la Roche show that in a vitiated and highly heated atmosphere the blood is not thoroughly decarbonized, thereby deranging the nervous system, and affecting the animal functions as well as the mental faculties. The blood is subject to incessant variations. The more feeble the respiration the less rich it is. Man absorbs twenty to thirty quarts of oxygen every hour. The pure air is a real food, and is as necessary for the development and repair of the physical force as the more solid forms of matter. Nine ounces of carbon are consumed every day, and the phenomenon of the expired carbonic acid has its maxima and minima during the day, like the regular variations of the barometer or the tides of the ocean.

v.

The great nervous prostration and the lack of energy which were observed among the prisoners, were not due entirely to climate. The activity of the nervous mechanism depends greatly upon the supply and purity of the arterial blood. It is the same with the nerve fibres as with the nerve centres, but in less degree. We observe that the exaltation and depression of the nervous power are within the control of man by the administration of certain drugs, or respiration of appropriate gases. The accumulation of bile or urea in the blood diminishes the nerve energy. Many physiologists enumerate moral depressions among the principal causes of epidemics; and this opinion is not strange when we consider how completely the system is under control of the nervous influence, and how much the supply of oxygen and blood to the organs and tissues depend upon the nervous power; and how much, moreover, the integrity of the nervous system depends upon the purity of the blood.

In the process of starvation, during the struggle for life, the hidden forces in reserve — the superabundant muscle, fat, tissues, even the brain-substance — are gradually absorbed. The volume of blood may remain the same, but the vivifying particles which circulate in the vital stream are rapidly consumed by the wants of the wasting economy, and disappear. And when these hematic globules are lessened to a certain limit below the normal proportion death ensues. Vierodt has discovered that the limit of this singular law is 52 per 1000 for the dog, and about 60 per 1000 for some other species of the mammalia. The physiologists have shown how the vivifying principles acquire vigor through the blood discs, and how these, when absorbing pure oxygen through the pulmonary circulation, contribute to the development of muscular fibre and the nervous material. Mammals and birds, when deprived of food, die in ten to twenty days, losing from one third to one half of their weight.

VI.

In determining the nutritive value of aliments by the study of their chemical composition, we cannot adhere strictly to the results furnished by analysis. For, says Baron Liebig, we cannot reckon upon results in the human stomach with the same regularity as we would in the alembics of our laboratories.

Physiologists divide alimentary substances into two classes: the nitrogenous, which, according to Dumas, supply the demands of assimilation, and the non-nitrogenous, which are called by Liebig respiratories, from furnishing the products consumed by respiration. Neither the one nor the other will alone support life indefinitely, and when one or the other decreases below well-defined limits, health declines, and finally life becomes extinct from inanition.

Milne Edwards gives, as the mean amount of these two classes, required for all climates, not less than three hundred and fifteen grains of nitrogen and thirty-three hundred and fifty grains of carbon in the twenty-four hours. These views are adopted by most physiologists; yet the analyses of Schlossberger and Kemp indicate that the idea of estimating the value of food by the quantity of nitrogen it contains is a fallacious one.

The beautiful experiments of Bernard and the modern physiologists have unfolded many of the laws that regulate digestion and assimilation. Yet the human researches in the great arcana of nature are extremely limited, in comparison with the vast range of physical phenomena, and every day we are reminded of the remarks of Boerhaave to his students: " Let all these heroes of science meet together; let them take bread and wine, the food which forms the blood of man, and by assimilation contributes to the growth of the body; let them try by all their art, and assuredly they will not be able from these materials to produce a single drop of blood, — so much is the most common act of nature beyond the utmost efforts of the most extended science."

The composition of the typical food of nature is revealed to us in the analysis of human milk.

VII.

The need of varied food is apparent to the casual observer, and it is well proven in the immortal work of Cabanis. " The experience of civilized life has shown," says Professor Horsford, in his admirable pamphlet on the marching ration of armies, " that the human organism requires, to maintain it in health, both organic and inorganic food.

" Of the organic, it needs nitrogenous food for the support of the vital tissues for work; and saccharine, or oleaginous food, for warmth. Of the inorganic, it needs phosphates for the bones, brain, muscles, and blood; and salt for its influence on the circulation and the secretions, and for various purposes where soda is required for a base; and doubtless both phosphates and salt for many offices as yet imperfectly understood. ' A man may be starved by depriving him of phosphates and salt, just as effectively as by depriving him of albumen or oil.' (Dalton's Physiology.)

" The salts of potassa, magnesia, and iron, of manganese, silica, and fluorine, are always present, and perform services of greater or less obvious moment in the animal economy. These organic and inorganic substances are essential, but they are not all that are needed. Man, especially when compelled to exhausting labor, requires beverages and condiments. He wants coffee, or tea, or cocoa; or, in the absence of these, he may feel a craving for wine or spirits. He wants salt, pepper, and vinegar. To preserve a sound body, then, there are required organic and inorganic food, beverages, and condiments."

" A mixed food," says another writer, " which varies from time to time, seems to be essential; and there can be no doubt that the changes which physicians have recognized in the nature of the predominating diseases, from century to century, are connected with changes which have taken place in the nature of the diet. Excess of oil, albumen, and starch produce liability to arthritic, bilious, and rheumatic affections; a deficiency of oleaginous materials, scrofula, &c."

VIII.

In attempting to form a proper estimate of the alleged ration furnished by the rebels to their prisoners at Andersonville, we will endeavor to arrive at just conclusions by comparing the known quantities with the dietaries of long-established hospitals, prisons, and the ration of armies of different periods of history.

The effects of food upon the civil prisoners, both of the long and short term, have been carefully studied by Christison, Liebig, Barral, and Edwards; and it is conclusively shown by their statistics of the prisons of Europe how much food will keep the prisoners in athletic condition when exposed to healthy influences. The quantity of food required depends upon the wants of the system and the quality of food consumed. Some articles are far more nutritious than others, and are far less bulky; for instance, the rice eaters of China, the potato and milk consumers of Ireland, eat enormously, compared with the beef-eating people.

But rarely will a less quantity than seventeen ounces suffice for the animal economy, and not then, even, unless it is the concentrated essences and principles of carefully selected grains, and healthy meat from cattle killed in their native pastures, like the scientific ration correctly proposed by Professor Horsford. This ration is intended to enable armies to change their base with intervals of more than a month, and to assist raiding parties to perform long journeys without relying for subsistence on the doubtful and difficult forage along the route, or on the distant depots at the point of departure.

A handful of the ripe, golden grains, roasted and mixed with a little sugar, with a few ounces of beef dried from the meat of healthy cattle killed instantly, will sustain the power of life wonderfully. This is shown by the mountaineers of the Cordilleras, of the Andes, and the Rocky Mountains.

It was substantially the same ration that enabled the Romans to traverse countries far remote from their main depots of supplies, and the Greeks to advance across, with safety, the immense arid deserts of Asia. Any of our splendidly equipped and fed armies of modern times would perish in a few days along the route where Xenophon and his immortal ten thousand passed with safety, and without much loss.

IX.

The mode of rationing the Roman armies, and the manner in which the supplies were obtained and preserved, is well shown in the extant writings of those times. Besides the allowance of wheat daily, — one to two pounds, — the Roman soldiers often received a ration of pork, mutton, legumes, cheese, oil, salt, wine, and vinegar. With the grain, a porridge-pot, a spit, the casque or a cup, and with vinegar to mix with their water, — which formed the regulation drink posea, or acetum, — they marched rapidly, and retained their extraordinary vigor in the midst of pestilential regions. Every soldier carried his own food for a given length of time, which was from eight to twenty-eight days. " *Cibo cum suo.*" Hence Josephus wrote, the Roman soldier is laden like a

mule. This food was always of the best quality; and
the wheat was always carefully selected by a commission
appointed for the purpose, as we may learn from the inscription on the column of Trajan. This wheat was not
always eaten raw; but was oftener roasted, and crushed
upon a stone.

> " Frugesque receptas
> Et torrere parant flammis et frugere saxo."

With all of these arrangements and movements, there
was method even as to the time of taking food. The
soldier ate twice a day, and at appointed hours — at the
sixth hour, " Prandium;" and at the tenth hour, " Ves-
perna."

x.

The requirements of the system differ greatly, according to the degree of heat, the purity of the air, and the
degree of physical exercise. What suffices at the equator would be but a morsel at the pole. What sustains
the quiet student would starve the active athlete.

When Volney spoke in surprise of the few ounces
required to sustain the Bedouin, he forgot the purity of
the air of the desert, as well as the indolent life of the
Arab.

When we offer as example the frugal diet of Cornaro,
which was twelve ounces of solid food, with fourteen
ounces of wine, daily, we must remember that the celebrated man lived a life of moderation, avoided bad air,
and guarded against the extremes of heat and cold.

The data of Frerichs, the observations of Sir John Sinclair, and the determinations of Professor Horsford, show that eighteen ounces of properly selected food may sustain life ; and they also show that the nutrient substances must be of known value.

XI.

In forming our ideas as to the required amount of food necessary to healthy vigor, we will not attempt to analyze the magnitudes of Lehman, nor accept the statement of Chossat, that the animal body loses daily about one twenty-fourth of its weight by the metamorphosis of tissue ; but will again examine the diet tables of the prisons, hospitals, and armies of Europe, leaving the reader to form his own conclusions.

The distinguished physiologist, Milne Edwards, maintains that the food must contain three hundred and fifteen grains of nitrogen and three thousand three hundred and fifty grains of carbon, otherwise the animal economy loses force, and gradually deteriorates. The data of Frerichs give the same views, and they accord with the observations of the ten years' study of the regimens of the prisons of Scotland. Dumas, in his calculations of the ration of the French army, gives as its equivalent three hundred and thirty-five grains of nitrogen and four thousand nine hundred and fifty grains of carbon.

In the prisons and hospitals of England, Scotland, France, and Germany, the dietaries furnish from seventeen to twenty-eight ounces of nitrogenous and carbonaceous food.

For a time, the solid ration of the prisons of Scotland

was reduced to seventeen ounces, but the prisoners lost weight. In the public institutions of England we find the total quantity of solid food to be as follows: The British soldier receives in home service 45 ounces; the seaman of the Royal navy 44 ounces; convicts 54 ounces; male pauper 29 ounces; male lunatic 31 ounces. The full diet of the hospitals of London furnish from 25 to 31 ounces of solid food, besides from one to five pints of beer daily. The Russian soldier has about 50 ounces; the Turkish more than 40 ounces; the French nearly 50 ounces; the Hessian 33 ounces; the Yorkshire laborer 50 ounces; United States navy 50 ounces; and the soldier of the United States army about 50 ounces, of solid food.

XII.

The food allowed to the prisoners at Andersonville, according to the statements of the prisoners and other witnesses, was from two to four ounces of bacon, and from four to twelve ounces of corn bread daily; sometimes a half pint to a pint of bean, pea, or sweet potato soup, of doubtful value. Vegetables were unknown. Thus giving a total weight of solid food, per diem, of six to sixteen ounces of solid food. The amount was not constant: some days the prisoners were entirely without food, as was the case at Belle Isle and Salisbury. Neither was the deficiency afterwards made good. The amount given was oftener less than ten ounces than more.

The contrast furnished by the dietaries of our own military prisons, of those of the British hulks (so much cursed during the last war), or by the food given by the

Algerine pirates to their prisoners and slaves, gives rise
:o terrible convictions as to the regard the rebel authori-
ies placed upon the lives of their prisoners. The United
States allowed to the rebel prisoners held by them thirty-
:ight ounces of solid food at first; but afterwards, in June,
1864, they reduced the ration to thirty-four and a half
)unces per day. The range of articles composing the
·ation was the same as with our own troops, the excep-
ion being in the weight in bread. In the Dartmoor
)rison in England, where our men were confined by the
English, when taken prisoners during the last war, and
)f which so much cruelty has been alleged, the authori-
ies allowed to the prisoners for the first five days in the
veek 24 ounces of coarse brown bread, 8 ounces of beef,
¼ ounces of barley, ⅓ ounce of salt, ⅓ ounce of onions,
ind 16 ounces of turnips daily (or more than 50 ounces
)f solid food); and for the remaining two days the usual
illowance of bread was given with 16 ounces of pickled
ish. The daily allowance to our men, at the Melville
Island prison, at Halifax, during the last war, was 16
)unces of bread, 16 ounces of beef, and one gill of peas;
he American agent furnishing coffee, sugar, potatoes, and
:obacco. The allowance on the noted Medway hulks
vas 8 ounces of beef, 24 ounces of bread, and one gill
)f barley, daily, for five days; and 16 ounces of codfish,
16 ounces potatoes, or 16 ounces of smoked herring, the
:emaining two days of the week. Furthermore, in addi-
:ion to these generous allowances of the British people,
t can be said that the quality of the food was almost
ilways excellent.

The writer, with one exception, knows of no dietary to

4 *

compare with that adopted, or made use of without the formality of adoption, by the rebel authorities in the treatment of their prisoners.

This exception is found in ancient history, which Plutarch has handed down to us. The Athenians, captured at the siege of Syracuse, were placed in the stone quarries of Ortygia, and fed upon one pint of barley and half a pint of water daily. Most of them perished from this treatment.

XIII.

The corn bread furnished was made, according to the evidence, from corn and the cob, ground up together, and sometimes mixed with what is called in the south cow peas. It varied from four to twelve ounces in weight daily, generally from four to eight ounces. A pound (of sixteen ounces) of corn bread contains, according to chemical analysis, two thousand eight hundred grains of carbon and one hundred and twenty-one grains of nitrogen, and therefore the highest quantity of corn bread furnished, say twelve ounces, afforded but two thousand one hundred grains of carbon and ninety grains of nitrogen, leaving a deficiency, according to the physiologists, of more than twelve hundred grains of carbon and two hundred grains of nitrogen, to be supplied by the two or four ounces of doubtful bacon.

That the bacon could not furnish this deficiency must be apparent to the scientific observer. The quantity of bread alone, required to furnish the desired amount of carbon and nitrogen, would have been over three pounds daily, which quantity the prisoners did not have.

Milne Edwards, after treating at length the subject of alimentation, and offering many examples, arrives at the conclusion that the mean quantity of bread and meat required to sustain the life of man, consists of sixteen ounces of bread and thirteen ounces of beef daily. This conclusion is sustained by most of the experimentalists, and if lesser quantities are used, they must be of choice selections. A small loaf of bread made of flour, ground from ripe, healthy wheat, will accomplish more for nutrition than two or three larger loaves, baked of damaged and unripe grain; and likewise it is with meat: half a pound of beef from cattle killed instantly in their native pastures, when the flesh retains all its natural juices and sweetness, is worth more for the support of the system than two or three pounds of beef from animals that have been fasted and terrified, and have thereby lost, in a very great measure, their nutritious qualities.

The flesh of mammalia undergoes a great change in its nutritive qualities by reason of fasting, disturbance of sleep, and long-continued suffering, resulting in its becoming not only worthless, but deleterious.

XIV.

Vegetable substances alone will not sustain life for a great length of time in every climate, but there is a vast difference between the wants of man at the equator and his necessities at the pole.

Nature requires for the working of her plans materials of diverse natures: neither the oil, nor starch, nor sugar, will sustain life alone. Chemical analysis and physiological history point out to us how positive is the law which fixes the component parts of grains and plants, and how imperative the necessity of adjusting in alimentation these forms of nutritive matter, which spring up on every side in profusion, and offer endless variety to the wants of man.

There must be harmony of certain principles; there must be union of starch, of gluten, and fat, to complete the process of digestion and assimilation. To feed a patient upon arrow-root, tapioca, or sago, and the like, is to consign him to certain death. Instinct impels us sometimes to make use of articles which our habits have thrown aside.

XV.

It appears from the reasoning of Baron Liebig, that when we replace the flesh and bread of ordinary diet by juicy vegetables and fruits, the blood is beyond all doubt altered in its chemical character, the alkaline carbonates being substituted for the phosphoric acid and alkaline phosphates, which are supposed to exert a disturbing influence in so many diseases, especially typhoid and inflammatory affections. The gluten of grain, and the albumen of vegetable juices, are identical in composition with the albumen of blood, but there are varieties of wheat, the ashes of which are in quantity and in relative proportion of the salts the same as those of boiled and lixiviated meats, and it cannot be maintained that bread made of such flour would, if it were the only food taken, support life permanently.

The experiments of the French academicians, show

that dogs fed exclusively on white bread, made from the sifted flour, died in forty days; but when fed on black bread (flour with the bran), they lived without disturbance of health. Bread should always be made of grains grown in healthy places, and should contain the entire seed, with the exception of the husk; then it will realize the idea of Paracelsus: "When a man eats a bit of bread, does he not therein consume heaven and earth, and all of the heavenly bodies, inasmuch as heaven by its fertilizing rain, the earth by its soil, and the sun by its luminous and heat-giving rays, have all contributed to its production, and are all present in the one substance?"

Desiccated vegetables, which have lost the water of vegetation and other gaseous elements, which chemistry thus far has been unable to discover, cannot adequately replace the fresh articles; the particular principle, the water of vegetation, can no more be restored to them than the dust of the crushed quartz can be recrystallized by the simple addition of water.

XVI.

In the alimentation of armies bread is the basal element. If it be poor, the whole system of the commissariat is deranged. History shows that it is the most important item in the feeding of soldiers, and that many a campaign, since the disaster to the army of Belisarius at Methon, has been lost in consequence of the quality of its munition bread.

France allows to her soldiers 26 ounces of bread, England 24, Belgium 28, Sardinia 26, Spain 23, Prussia 32,

Austria 32, Turkey 33, United States 22, *Rebel Prisons* 4 *to* 12 *ounces!*

The quantity of corn meal allowed to the rebel soldiers by the rebel government was about one and one-third pounds daily : this would give about 28 ounces of bread, allowing 30 per cent. of water, which is the rule among bakers ; at least it is the average quantity established by the civil tax commission of Paris. Besides the corn meal they had six ounces of bacon, and peas, and rice. This ration was sufficient to preserve life, as it has been shown by the condition of the rebel armies ; the bread alone contained 4900 grains of carbon, and 210 grains of nitrogen, without the aid of bacon or the peas. The bread alone has an excess of 1600 grains of carbon, and a deficiency only of about 100 grains of nitrogen, which was readily supplied by the bacon and other articles. Corn bread is one of the chief articles of diet in the Southern States, and it is likewise used extensively in the South of Europe. It makes heavy bread unless carefully prepared and mixed with flour, and when mixed with the cob it often produces a laxative effect, the degree of which depends greatly upon the quantity the meal contains. When properly prepared with milk and the usual ingredients, it becomes an agreeable and nutritious article of diet, but carelessly handled, it is disagreeable to the palate and difficult to digest.

The bread furnished to the prisoners was simply mixed with salt and the dirty water from the brook, or the foul spring in the rear of the bakery, and then dried in the heat of the oven. That bad effects arose from such a quality of bread cannot be doubted ; the injurious influences of impure water in panification have been pointed out by Boussingault, in a paper presented to the French Academy in 1857.

It is the common saying in the Southern States, where the use of wheaten bread is comparatively rare, that a bushel of corn contains more nutriment than a bushel of wheat. Yet the southern wheat is superior to the northern varieties, and is richer in the azotized, glutinous principles so essential to the formation of blood and muscle. Vermicelli and macaroni can be made only from the best southern wheat.

Of the varieties of Indian corn in America, the yellow flinty corn is reckoned the sweetest and most nutritive; the white corn of the South makes the fairest, but considerably the weakest flour. We do not find special fault with the coarsely ground meal, provided the cob is not included, for Mayer has pointed out, in discarding the commercial bran we throw away fourteen times as much phosphoric acid as there is in superfine flour. In this bran are contained most of the layers of gluten, in which are lodged the phosphates and the companion nitrogenous compounds — the sources of living tissues. The nutritious Graham bread is an example; also the pumpernickel of Westphalia, the black bread of Russia, the coarse oatmeal of Scotland, contain all the gluten, all the phosphates and nitrogenous compounds, as well as the starch of the grains. Such was the bread that Celsus considered as equal to flesh in its capacity of nourishing.

XVII.

, Fresh meat was rarely furnished to the prison, according to the reports and statements of witnesses, and we should doubt that it was furnished at all, if it were not for the number of sections of the horns of cattle which are strewn about the enclosure, and which the prisoners had used for drinking dishes; still, many of these horns may have been taken from the cattle killed for the guards.

That the issue of fresh beef would have been beneficial to the men, there is no doubt; in fact, the experiment at Jamaica, which continued twenty years, proves it; for the troops who were fed with a larger allowance of fresh meat suffered far less from dysentery than any of the troops of the West India islands. There is always great difficulty in preserving the good qualities of fresh meat in hot climes, and, on the other hand, the use of salt meat in the same regions is apt to engender scorbutic disorders. Whenever putrefactive fermentation begins with any kind of meat, or any recently living nitrogenized substance, catalytic action takes place, ammonia is evolved, and the product is no longer pleasant to the taste or nutritious to the system. Food, when even exposed to vitiated air, becomes deteriorated in quality, just as good flour is rendered worthless by mixture with the damaged fungoid grain. Butchers' meat on the average affords but thirty-five per cent. of real nutritive matter, at least such was the opinion presented to the French Minister of the Interior by Vauquelin and Percy. Accepting this determination, we may form some idea of the relative value of the scanty allowance of the doubtful beef furnished to the prisoners, if it was furnished at all.

That bacon was furnished, there is no doubt; neither has the quantity been underrated by the sufferers themselves, as we shall presently see. And there is no reason why the quality should not have been most excellent, unless it had been selected for the purposes of cruelty. There is evidence that it was sometimes of very bad quality; but that it was generally and systematically selected to disgust the prisoners, we are unwilling to believe, although we have evidence that rotten bacon was furnished by contractors, and the fact boasted of by them. The influence and effect of this decomposed food may be surmised by the following remark of Donovan: 'Flesh contains the elements of some of the most deadly poisons that are found even in the vegetable kingdom; a slight change in their mode of combination, or of the ratio of their quantities, may convert nutriment into a source of death."

XVIII.

There is another very important item to be considered in the dietary of this prison, and that is the quality and quantity of the water furnished for potable purposes. 'Water," says Milne Edwards, " is an aliment, as well as sugar and fibrine; for it is indispensable for the nutrition of the body, and, by whatever means it arrives in the economy, its *rôle* is always the same."

The water consumed in the prison was obtained from the brook, and from the few wells or springs within the stockade. The volume of water in the brook was quite sufficient to furnish all the drinking water desired, if it had been introduced into the stockade by means of sluices. As it was, the course of the stream was left to nature, and no effort made to prevent its defilement by the camps situated farther up, or by the bake-house located close by. All the camps on the declivities about Andersonville were drained into this stream. Some few wells were sunk in the prison which yielded scanty supplies, and there were also a few springs undefiled; but the quality of water everywhere was surface water, tinged and tainted with the impurities of the soil and the infections of the collected filth. The thirst, which was excessive among the prisoners, could only be slaked by drinking the impure waters. Yet a very little care on the part of the rebel authorities would have increased the comfort of the prisoners in this respect, and prevented the loss of life to a very considerable degree.

" The preservation of potable water," writes Felix Jacquot, " is certainly one of the capital points of hygiene."

" I am sometimes disposed to think," states Dr. Letheby, the health officer of London, " that impure water is before impure air as one of the most powerful causes of disease." In cold climates slight impurities in the drinking water are not of vital importance; but in the tropics, and the adjacent regions, the least decayed vegetable or animal matter renders it injurious and unpalatable, and often is the determining cause of disease, especially enteric, to a fearful degree.

XIX.

During the months of June, July, August, and September, 1864, there was an aggregate number of prisoners of about twenty-eight thousand for each month. To supply this vast number of men with bread would have been ordinarily no easy task, requiring, as it would have done, twenty-eight thousand rations of bread daily, or eight hundred and forty thousand rations monthly. We have shown that the bakery could not have furnished more than ninety-six hundred rations of corn bread, of the United States weight of twenty ounces, or ninety-six hundred rations daily, or two hundred and eighty-eight thousand rations monthly, and probably furnished but five thousand rations daily, or one hundred and fifty thousand rations monthly. If this deficiency of a half a million of rations existed, how can it be explained ?

Was munition bread brought from a distance to supply the deficiency? When and whence, we will ask?

During the period embracing the months of July, August, and September, 1864, the rebel commissary furnished, according to his statements, two hundred and twenty-three thousand bushels of corn meal, and thirty-even hundred bushels of flour for the prison.

There was, during this time (ninety-two days), a monthly aggregate of twenty-nine thousand prisoners, who required twenty-nine thousand rations of corn meal daily ; or, multiplied by ninety-two days, two million six hundred and sixty-eight thousand rations for the period of three months ; or, allowing the same weight as the rebel ration, we have $2,668,000 \times 1\frac{1}{3} = 3,567,333$ pounds of

corn meal, or seventy-one thousand one hundred and
forty-six bushels, allowing fifty pounds to the bushel. If
we now estimate the rebel garrison to have been four
thousand in the aggregate, we will have for the re
quirements, 4000 $\times$ 92 $\times$ $1\frac{1}{2}$ = 552,000 pounds of meal
or ten thousand one hundred and ninety bushels, which
gives, as total for the prison and garrison, eighty-one
thousand two hundred and eighty-six bushels of corn
meal.

Yet the commissary states that he sent two hundred
and twenty-three thousand bushels, or almost three time
as much as the quantity required. This is a strange
statement to make, as we shall endeavor to show.

The rebel ration allowed by their law gave thirty-seven
and a half pounds of corn meal, three pounds of rice, or
five pounds of peas, ten pounds of bacon, salt, &c.
monthly, of twenty-eight days, or about twenty ounces of
meal daily, and about six ounces of bacon. We have
as an aggregate number of men for the above period
(prisoners and guards), 29,000 + 4000 $\times$ 92 = 3,036,000
men, requiring, according to law, three million seven
hundred and ninety-five thousand pounds of corn meal
Now the commissary states that he furnished 226,700
bushels of corn meal and flour; or, multiplied by 50
pounds = 11,335,000 pounds, thus giving to each man
more than three and one-fifth pounds of meal and
flour; or, allowing the usual per cent. of water, more
than four pounds of bread. That these men had sixty
eight ounces of corn bread apiece, or that they could
have eaten it if they had been furnished that quantity
is not for a moment to be considered. This analysis

)etrays the falsity of the commissary's statement, and nvalidates the remainder of his accounts.

It cannot be said that this meal was to be stored for uture use, for it is well known that corn meal will not keep in this climate but for a few days without fermentaion taking place. There is, again, another serious item o be considered in connection with this statement. Why should this overplus, of more than seven millions of pounds of meal, be sent to this prison, when the army of Virginia was calling loudly for grain? The statement and the figures indicate simply a foolish desire to cover up deficiencies, and that too in a very hasty manner.

XX.

The same commissary states that he sent, during the same period of time, three hundred and thirty-nine thousand pounds of bacon, or five million four hundred and twenty-four thousand ounces. This will give thirty-six hundred and eighty-four pounds of bacon each day of the ninety-two days; and, after allowing six ounces per man to the rebel garrison, we shall have remaining but two thousand pounds to be divided among the twenty-nine thousand prisoners, or about one and one seventh ounces of bacon to each man. Thus the account of the commissary, if true, proves that the statement of the prisoners, that they received but two to four ounces of bacon daily, was correct.

If the full amount of bacon had been allowed, there would have been required, at the rate of six ounces per man, ten thousand eight hundred and seventy-five pounds daily, whereas there was in reality but two thousand pounds, leaving a deficiency of more than eight thousand pounds daily. If fresh beef had been allowed at the same rate as the bacon, there would have been required ten thousand eight hundred and seventy-five pounds daily, or a herd of thirty of the native cattle, allowing three hundred and sixty pounds net weight to each carcass. If the full ration of one pound of fresh beef had been furnished there would have been required more than one hundred and twenty of the same class of cattle daily.

XXI.

That the dietary of the prisoners was far from being adequate to their wants there is no doubt, and it only remains to be determined whether this deficiency arose from design, from ignorance, or from real scarcity of food

We have very serious doubts as to the truth of the statements that there was a scarcity of food in this vicinity during the time of the occupation of the prison.

At the time of its selection the region was considered to be the richest in cereals of all the Southern States.

In times previous it had proved to be fertile, and during the progress of the war the slave labor was undisturbed by the Federal troops. It is shown by their own statistics that in 1860 the four counties near the prison, and along the line of railroad, produced nearly fourteen hundred thousand bushels of corn, thirty-three thousand bushels of wheat, three hundred thousand bushels of potatoes, and more than one hundred thousand bushels of beans and peas, besides forty-eight thousand bales of cotton.

It is highly probable that these quantities were doubled, if not trebled and quadrupled during the succeeding years of the war, when the planting of cotton was forbidden by rebel ukase, and all energy and labor were turned to the production of food. There were in these four counties alone more than twenty thousand slaves.

In the south of Georgia, in the wire-grass region, were great numbers of cattle roaming at will, and the numbers in the everglades of Florida were so vast, that two old steamboat captains offered to furnish the rebel government, at this very period, with half a million pounds of salt beef, along the railroads in Florida. Governor Watts wrote from Alabama in April, 1864, that there were ten million pounds of bacon accessible in that State. In September of the same year, Mr. Hudson, of the adjoining State of Alabama, offered to deliver to the rebel government half a million pounds of bacon in exchange for the same quantity of cotton.

The rebel war clerk, in his diary at Richmond, wrote, March 17, 1864, " It appears that there is abundance of grain and meat in the country ; " and again, July 3, 1864, he notes down, " Our crop of wheat is abundant, and the harvest is over."

According to the census of 1860, there were in Florida more than six hundred thousand cattle and swine, and more than five millions in Georgia and Alabama. These two States produced during the same year more than sixty million bushels of corn and thirteen million bushels of potatoes. (Vide Appendix.)

XXII.

As to the arrangement for the distribution of the food, there was but little attention paid to system. The prisoners were ordered to arrange themselves into squads of two hundred and ninety men, and these squads were then subdivided into three messes. None of these messes appear to have been properly supplied with utensils to receive and distribute their food. Every prisoner was obliged to take care of himself, and all around the area of the stockade may be seen at the present day remains of bent pieces of tinned iron, the rudely-fashioned little

tub, and sections of the horns of cattle which the poor prisoners had worked up with their knives, and utilized for their necessities. Civilized men would never have resorted to these primitive, rough, and slovenly means, if they had been supplied with the ordinary utensils. At certain hours carts, laden with the corn bread and bacon, were driven into the enclosure, and the rations were distributed right and left. When soup was made, it was brought in pails, and the prisoners received it in their horn cups, wooden tubs, or as best they could. No drink was allowed but the water from the brook, whose ripples were like the river Lethe, for they contained the elements of oblivion and death.

XXIII.

It is evident to the writer that the quantity of food furnished to the prisoners was far from being adequate to support animal life, and from this deficiency alone he can explain to his satisfaction the enormous loss of life. The admirable experiments of Boussingault and the French academicians show how the increase of weight in the feeding of animals is in direct proportion to the amount of plastic constituents in the daily supply of food, and how positive is the law which regulates the animal economy. Again, we can form some idea of the positive effects of the horrible condition of the prison, and of the extremes of heat and moisture upon the feeble digestion and assimilation, by the experiments of Claude Bernard, who shows how these functions may be disturbed by external influences, and how agony even causes the disappearance of sugar in the hepatic organ, and how fear disturbs the glucogenic process. There is connected with inanition a singular tendency to decomposition and putridity, alike in the blood and viscera. The system left unnourished rapidly wastes, and its vitality soon lessens to a degree beyond recovery. This degree depends upon the forces in reserve, which belongs especially to youth ; middle age is less liable to impressions, but when once affected, has less support from the system. The rapidity with which the dead decomposed immediately after death, astonished the observing surgeon.

The prevailing diarrhœa and scorbutic condition were the results of the want of food and the combined influences of the bad air and water, and not the primary causes of the feebleness and death.

The effect of the want of food first appears in loss of color — wasting away of the form, diminution of strength, vertigo, relaxation of the system of the viscera as well as of the muscles, diarrhœa appears, and rapidly closes the struggle of the natural forces for life.

A few days, or a few weeks, according to the initial condition, is sufficient to test the tenacity of the powers of life. Death always takes place whenever the diminution of the total weight of the body reaches certain limits, which is from from $\frac{40}{100}$ to $\frac{50}{100}$ of the usual weight. We observe this law to be quite positive and regular with the lower animals, with whom the effect of starvation has been well studied, and the limit of loss, compatible with life, found to be $\frac{40}{100}$ for mammals and $\frac{50}{100}$ for birds.

BOOK FIFTH.

" Les Hôpitaux. C'est ici que l'humanité en pleurs accuse les for-
faits de l'ambition."

I.

THE Hospital is the recognized type of mercy, in its broadest range of benevolence, tenderness, and compassion, all over the countries of the earth, wherever the noble sentiments of nature have force. It is one of the emblems of the great religion of civilization. It is coeval with Christ, for it appeared among the institutions of men in definite shape only after the establishment of Christianity ; and to its true exalting effects upon the dispositions of men, the Christian religion owes in great measure its rapid progress among the barbarous and pagan nations of the earth.

In earlier times public charity was rare or impulsive among the civil communities. It was only the suffering and disabled defenders of the general service who were cared for at the expense of the state, as at the Prytaneum among the Athenians, or the numerous asylums which munificent Rome erected to the brave men who carved out with their strong arms and their blades of steel the colossal forms of her glory and grandeur. The magnificent ruins of Italica, which sheltered the disabled veterans and heroes of Africanus, look down at the pres-

with which th^e vast and fertile plains of the Guadalquivir,
astonished t' later and higher civilizations with neglect and
    The p^ide.
the r^
flu^   II.

But it is to the beneficent and sublime influences of
Christianity that are to be attributed the noble institutions
of the present day, where the suffering and infirm receive
the attentions of science and the consolations of humanity.

Never among civilized nations are they profaned for the
purposes of cruelty, never defiled by murder under the
mask of philanthropy.

Enlightened communities vie with each other in self-
sacrifice in the great and heroic labor of devotion to
suffering mortality. It is the distinguishing degree of
difference in their excellence, their refinement, their
religion.

It is the last thought and reflection of the dying man,
who, in dividing his worldly material with charity and
benevolence, hopes to be kindly remembered on earth.
It is the first dawning idea of childhood, with its infant
hands filled with roses and garlands of flowers to relieve
the pains of human suffering, or adorn the pale features
of the departed.

To delight in human misery is the last degree of
earthly degradation and perversity. The mockery of the
agony of death belongs only to the fiends of hell and
their baser imitators.

III.

Not until some time after the occupation of the prison did the care and condition of the sick attract the attention and excite the solicitude of the prison-keepers. Then a space was selected to the eastward, and almost adjoining the stockade, and here were pitched the decayed and dilapidated tents which were to form the hospital.

The exact size of the space is not known, the boundaries having disappeared since the evacuation; but the tents were arranged, it is said, with some degree of regularity, and the collection was surrounded by a fence, which served only to obstruct the circulation of free air, which was of vital importance; and besides, the fence was of no service whatever as protection against the escape of the inmates, as they were before admission generally far too feeble to make even an effort.

The actual amount of accommodation furnished is not known. By some it is stated that there were nothing whatever but a few rotten tent flies; by others, and among them one of the surgeons, it is narrated that there were tents to cover one thousand men, and three large kettles to provide for their cooking, and nothing more. Yet the records show that there were nearly four thousand men at one time in this hospital. This distribution of the means for the protection and sustenance of life is too terrible to be believed. Let us overlook it, for there is sufficient for execration elsewhere, without turning to the more revolting violation and desecration of one of the sanctuaries of civilization.

Beneath these tent covers there was neither straw, nor

mattresses, nor bunks: there was simply the bare earth, with no protection but what was afforded by the rotten canvas, the scanty clothing, the ragged blanket, which the hapless sufferer might possess. Many of the unfortunate men who perished here had neither shelter nor clothing. The rapacity of the captors had taken the remnants of the rags left by the fury of battle. For this want of shelter, and couches to protect and rest the weary limbs, there is no excuse, and there can be none; for in the adjoining forests there were immense quantities of timber accessible, and easy of conversion into manufacture, and the extremities of the boughs of the long-leaved or Southern pine afforded the means of making comfortable and healthy beds.

There were then within the stockade many thousands of men accustomed to the use of the axe, the adze, the saw, and the plane, who would have in few days fashioned implements of steel out of the useless scraps of railway iron lying at the depot, and transformed the forest into vast, even magnificent buildings, replete with the comforts, the conveniences of advanced art. There were artisans here, of education and ingenuity, who could have formed out of the very dust of the place edifices as beautiful and wonderful to the imagination and understanding as the reality was repulsive and strange.

IV.

The guards furnished themselves with comfortable huts, arranged with the common conveniences, and their bunks were suspended above the contact of the treacherous ground. Their invalids were well cared for also in the large hospital which was erected expressly for the garrison, and which consisted of two large two-story wooden buildings, admirably arranged, with the conveniences proper to the service. The kitchen, the dispensary, the ventilation, and the general arrangement, showed that scientific care and forethought had been observed there.

The hospital system of the rebels was quite complete, and most of their hospitals throughout the country were well constructed and equipped; and some of them were models of neatness, comfort, and scientific arrangement.

The garrison hospital at Andersonville offers a terrible contrast to the open space, the wretched agglomeration, which the rebel authorities called a hospital for the prisoners.

It is true that the commanding officers were compelled, from some unknown pressure, — whether the sense of shame, or dictate from Richmond, — to order and commence the erection, at a late date, of a new hospital stockade. This was to consist of a high palisade, about one thousand feet in length, with twenty-two open sheds erected in the interior; but it was never finished, nor occupied, and it remains to-day as it was left by the rude, black artisans, one of the evidences of either remorse or reluctant obedience to the lingering sense of natural compassion of its senseless and heartless rulers.

v.

In the organization of a hospital the most important parts are the system of nursing and the supply and cooking of food; when these are observed, much exposure to the elements can be endured.

Pestilences are retarded, and sometimes completely checked, in their destructive career when opposed by generous alimentation and sympathetic care; and the vital powers, — the *vis medicatrix naturæ*, — rally their mighty strength for renewed effort. We have for instance the great and marked change in the healthy condition and the mortality of the British army before Sebastopol in the spring of 1856, when England poured out lavishly her treasures, and sent men of scientific ability to correct the well-nigh fatal errors of hygiene which were committed by her military men.

We have also another instance in the check of a devastating pestilence at New Orleans, as observed and mentioned by Dr. Cartwright. "As soon as a generous public diffused the comforts of life among the seventy thousand destitute emigrant population of New Orleans, last summer, the pestilence, which was sweeping into eternity three hundred a day, immediately began to disappear, before frost or any other change in the weather, its artificial fabric being broken down by the beneficent hand of the American people."

VI.

Here there appears to have been neither system, nor order, nor humanity. The chances of recovery were far less than the certainty of death. In reality, it was almost certain death; for only twenty-four out of the hundred who entered ever returned to the prison again. Those patients who possessed sufficient strength helped themselves to what was at hand, and what was afforded by the meagre dietary; those who had not, folded their arms and died.

Medical men went through the formality of prescribing for the dying men, but with formulæ whose ingredients were unknown to them.

Some of these surgeons gloated over the distresses of their fellow-men, and delighted in the awful destruction of life which was branding with eternal infamy the manhood of their nation.

Others turned and wept, for humanity was not extinct. Those tears have in part blotted out and redeemed the fearful inscriptions in that record of the events of life which form the history of the human race.

It is not known that woman ever visited these precincts from feelings of compassion, and, offered to console the last moments of the dying. We do know that they gazed upon the scene from a distance, but with what emotion history wisely makes no note.

In Catholic countries we observe the hospitals attended by nuns, sisters of mercy and charity, all eager to labor in behalf of humanity. Besides these, the deaconesses of the Rhine and the beguines of Flanders have acquired an imperishable record in history for their philanthropic efforts. "There is is nothing," says Voltaire, "nobler than the sight of delicate females sacrificing beauty, youth, often wealth and rank, to devote themselves to the relief of human miseries under the most revolting forms." We have seen in our own time, in the hospitals of the Federal armies, a devoted band of self-sacrificing women

5 *

striving to perform their part in the great work of philanthropy. Here woman never appeared. There were, in reality, only the vivid· impressions of horror, complaints, groans, delirium, and the agony of death.

More than eight thousand of our men perished miserably in this neglected and iniquitous spot.

Men were seen here in all stages of idiocy and imbecility from the effects of starvation. They were seen asking for bones to gnaw to relieve the pangs of hunger. Compassion never will believe that this request was made by dying mortals, and that too in a hospital, which is regarded among men as the holy institution of society, and even by infuriated combatants as the only sacred precinct on the brutal fields of war.

The same wail of distress was heard on the plains of Texas, and along the military lines of Virginia.

Thus the black flag, threatened by the rebel cabinet, was hoisted. Without the courage to proclaim their intentions openly and boldly upon the battle-field, they exhibited them in as sure, but different form, in the management of their prisons.

VII.

The stories relating to vaccination with poisonous matter are doubtless untrue. That there were disastrous effects from vaccination is probably correct, but they must have been the results of accident. Similar consequences have been observed in civil communities, in armies, and in hospitals. Serious results have been noticed by the writer in our own armies and hospitals.

Vaccine matter is extremely liable to decomposition; and when heated, even by the warmth of the body, fermentation arises, and by catalytic action putrefaction results, forming a positive poison. That the directors of this hospital should resort to such means for the destruction of human life is not at all probable, for the process required labor: and besides, the wretched invalids died with sufficient rapidity without the intervention of this new art of malice.

VIII.

In all military hospitals, food is to be regarded as the principal medicament. With good food, the results of surgery may be foretold with tolerable certainty, and the obstructions to the medical treatment lessen greatly or disappear. Without the aid of pure, healthful, life-giving aliment, the duration of animal life is always brief when when exposed to vicious and hostile influences.

The ration used here, or the system of dietary, was not constant; neither do we know sufficiently well the quantity, or quality, or variety, to form a true and candid estimate of its value in sustaining the physical strength, or repairing the waste and metamorphose of the organs and tissues of the system.

We know, however, that it was supposed to be bacon, flour, and corn bread — rarely fresh meat; and vegetables were almost unknown. The only vegetables and delicacies were either obtained in exchange, at exorbitant rates, for the little currency which the prisoners had managed to secrete among their rags, or they were now and then introduced stealthily by a few of the humane surgeons at the peril of their lives. Persons whose systems are weakened by want of proper food, by exhaustion from excessive labor, or exposure, or disease, require a great variety of articles from which to select the substances which a depraved but instinctive palate often craves. Food which would disgust the healthy appetite, will not quicken into action the debilitated and flickering sensation of taste. During an enfeebled condition, loathsome morsels become injurious; for digestion is clearly at the command of the mind, and is often checked by its caprices.

IX.

The effect of gentle care and kindly sympathy is more felt, more marked in the military hospitals, than in the civil. Home is farther away, and the sense of loneliness which all invalids experience is far more oppressive. Here it is that woman's influence is the strongest, and her sweet disposition, her friendly, compassionate smile, seems to prolong life, and put to flight the advancing shadows of death. " It is not medicine," says Charles Lamb; " it is not broth and coarse meats served up at stated hours with all the hard formality of a prison; it is not the scanty dole of a bed to lie on which a dying man requires from his species. Looks, attentions, consolations, in a word, sympathies, are what a man most needs in this awful close of human sufferings. A kind look, a smile, a drop of cold water to a parched lip — for these things a man shall bless you in death."

With soldiers, these little attentions have great effect;

partly from the law of contrast with the roughness of their every-day occupations and life, and partly from the rarity of such influences. And finally, when grim Death appears, there is with them a singular philosophy, calmness, and resignation. The writer has observed this upon many battle-fields, and in the hospitals far removed. Rarely do we hear lamentations, regrets, and shrieks for help: the conscious man folds his arms, and resigns himself to his inward thoughts, thinking, perhaps, of

> " His native hills that rise in happier climes,
> The grot that heard his song of other times,
> His cottage home, his bark of slender sail,
> His glassy lake, and broomwood blossomed vale."

X.

The forms of disease observed here were simple, and they seldom exhibited positive indications, or, rather, the immediate effects and influences of malaria. Neither of the four great pestilential diseases appeared — cholera, yellow fever, plague, or remittent fever.

The diseases treated, or noted down rather upon the hospital register, were generally the different forms of inanition, or of exhaustion of the powers of life by the absorption of noxious vapors, or by the exposure when in feeble condition to the extremes of heat and moisture.

The mortality among the patients removed to this place was perfectly appalling. Nearly eight hundred men out of every thousand perished. Yet this might have been foretold from the horrible condition, the pre-arranged destitution of the hospital. Besides carefully selected food, pure and dry air is indispensable for the recovery of a diseased condition, and damp and vitiated air is sure to retard improvement, or to induce complications.

Neither food nor healthy atmosphere were afforded.

The symptoms of the patients indicated the want of food, and were not in reality the signs of actual disease. And the post-mortems made at this hospital revealed the absence of lesion, save those consequent upon starvation or prolonged suffering.

The minutes of this clinic are very extensive and particular, and they exhibit in overwhelming proof the cause of death.

Life was prolonged to the last degree of the natural vitality, and among the phenomena observed, the law of muscular irritability, as discovered and explained by Brown-Sequard, was well illustrated. There was no cadaveric rigidity; for the want of nutrition, the vitiated atmosphere, the exposure to the vicissitudes of climate, had weakened and utterly destroyed all nervous power. Immediately after the cessations of the functions of life, putrefaction appeared and progressed with great rapidity.

XI.

In discussing the rate of mortality of this hospital, we cannot with propriety assume a standard for comparison, for nowhere can we turn to analyze results from similar causes. We may, perhaps, take the data and statistics of our own military prisons, but the contrasts are too fearful for credulity. We will consider these at length, with other comparisons, in the next Book.

"The truth is in the facts, and not in the spirit that
udges them."

XII.

The want of system cannot be charged to the fault of
he organization of the rebel Bureau of Medicine, for
hat was well arranged and strictly governed.

It may partly be ascribed to the general carelessness of
he officers in charge, and partly to the desire of the
ulers that the numbers of prisoners should decrease, and
onsequently their labors should diminish, no matter how,
ior how quickly.

That there were men in charge of the patients who
vere destitute of all moral scruples, of all refined and
iumane sentiments, there can be no doubt, but there were
ι few men who did not partake of the general madness
if the spirit of destruction, and who exhibited a tender
egard for the sufferings of their fellow-men. The names
if Thornberg and Head will always be preserved as
imong the only few redeeming acts in the story of the
great wrong. The sympathy of these men was undisguised, and when protest failed to produce kindly impres-
ions, or to bring alleviation to misery, they secretly sought
o succor the dying men from their own scanty store at
he peril of their lives.

Dr. Head was not only threatened with death by the
rutal Wirz, but he was actually imprisoned for a short
ime for giving to the dying some vegetables which he had
gathered from his little garden. "Sire," said the noble
Surgeon Larry to Napoleon, "it is my avocation to pro-
ong life, and not to destroy it."

Let no man attempt to recall the scenes that took place in this wretched enclosure, which was falsely called a hospital; let no man attempt to lift the veil of darkness which now obscures the acts or the animus which governed and directed this mockery of philanthropy, for the human mind already staggers under the load of horror which is imposed by the events of every-day life, and advanced civilization has no desire to renew the recollection of the atrocities of the dark ages.

BOOK SIXTH.

"To die, is the common lot of humanity. In the grave, the only distinction lies between those who leave no trace behind and the heroic spirits who transmit their names to posterity." — *Tacitus.*

I.

IT is always difficult to determine the natural duration of life, or the death-rate for any locality or any class of people, since the range of circumstances that affect the health of men and animals is so vast, that it requires great research, powers of analysis and comparison ; so extensive a knowledge of the phenomena and the laws of life, that few men have the courage to attack, or the ability to comprehend and solve the complex problem.

In our estimations we must consider what is due to the agencies of the natural world, such as geology, meteorology, and the like, as well as to age, constitution, temperament, anterior professions, and morbid predispositions, also the exaltation and demoralization of moral action.

"We see," says Buffon, "that man perishes at all ages, while animals appear to pass through the period of life with firm and steady pace." The great naturalist shows how the passions, with their attendant evils, exercise great influence upon the health, and derange the principles which sustain us; how often men lead a nervous and contentious life, and that most of them die of disappointment. Buffon is right, and the English statistics show us that the duration of life is generally in proportion to its happiness and regularity, and that miserable lives are soon extinguished.

Hope sometimes forsakes the stoutest hearts, and with hope disappears the mainspring of earthly life.

II.

In deciding upon the causes of the excessive mortality at Andersonville, there is not much obscurity to contend with. But we must admit that there must have been some mortality, for there is a determined duration of life for every species of animal; and we must also allow that under the most favorable circumstances, the death-rate of soldiers encamped in this unhealthy locality would have been far beyond the normal limit.

From calculations based upon the most accurate and extensive observations made in England for a long series of years, it was determined that a mortality of less than two per cent. per annum for all ages might be assumed as a fair average rate of deaths in a population where sanitary measures were properly attended to.

It is noticed by eminent observers, that the mean rate for Europe is about three per cent.; which is regarded as excessive, being about double of what is estimated as the natural ratio.

Our distinguished statistician, Dr. Edward Jarvis, remarks that the mortality of two per cent. in England includes all ages — infancy as well as the last decades of life; and he states that the proper rates for comparison are those of the males in England of the military age, which is observed to be less than one per cent.

He shows that the death-rate of the soldier in England is less than one per cent., and also considers the stated mortality of three per cent. for the continent of Europe as much too high. The mortality on the continent is greater than in England, and greater in England than in Scotland.

In times of peace, the mortality of soldiers is not much greater than that of the civil laborers; but during campaigns no limit can properly be given, for the vicissitudes are so rapid, and the exposures so varied, that the chances of life and death cannot be estimated with fairness, or with any degree of certainty. But when encampments are arranged, and occupied for any considerable length of time, the possibilities and probabilities of health may then be considered with propriety.

III.

These chances and these causes of general mortality depend upon the atmospheric influences, the mephitism of the soil, the density of the population, and the excellence of the food and shelter, as well as upon the natural vigor and strength of the individual.

Some classes of human beings have greater tenacity of life than others, but all are affected by vicious influences, and yield sooner or later to the elements of destruction. "Everything in the animal economy is regulated by fixed and positive laws."

" We live on our forces," says Galen : " as long as our
forces are sound, we can resist everything ; when they become weak, a trifle injures us."   The truth of this remark
is well illustrated in the life of the soldier, whose health
is in exact ratio to the condition in which he is placed.
And his mode of existence, the combined influence of
food, exposure, and the training of mind and body, give
a peculiar character, which requires, when disabled,
special modification of treatment, and a particular kind of
experience.   The ancient physiologists distinguished two
kinds, or rather two provisions of strength — the forces
in reserve and the forces in use ; or, as they said, " Vires
in posse et vires in actu ; " or, as Barthez describes it, the
radical forces and the acting forces.

The young soldier, supported by this buoyancy of the
unknown force of life, recovers from terrible shocks and
disasters to his system, while the old man, fatigued and
exhausted by the great and protracted labors of active
campaigns, feels that he has the hidden resources — the
reserved and superabundant powers of youth — no longer.

IV.

" The atmospheric influences, the mephitism of the
soil, and the inhabited locality, are the three principal
conditions of the causes of general mortality," says
Pringle.

He should have added food ; for diet, of all external
causes, affects the condition of the human race more than
any other.   Those who have observed the mortality curve
follow the harvests in Ireland and Germany, and noticed

how strangely the number of the dead corresponded to the scantiness of food, and those who have experimented with the feeding of domesticated animals, will agree with me on this point.

Let us review these three great principles of destruction, as laid down by the distinguished European authority, and apply them in the explanations of the mortality at Andersonville.

v.

It has been observed by medical men, from the time of Hippocrates down to the present day, that the effects of a heated atmosphere, saturated with moisture, are very injurious, and exceedingly prolific of disease.

Air at 32° of Fahrenheit, according to Leslie, contains, when saturated with moisture, $\frac{1}{160}$ of its weight of water; at 59°, $\frac{1}{80}$; at 86°, $\frac{1}{40}$; at 113°, $\frac{1}{20}$; its capacity for moisture being doubled by each increase of 27° of Fahrenheit.

The degree of heat within the stockade sometimes rose to beyond 110° Fahrenheit, and the degree of humidity was correspondingly as great. That moisture exerts more influence in the production of disease than any other meteorological condition, is well observed in everyday life. M. Bossi found, in his investigations, that the extreme and constant humidity of the atmosphere affected the barometer of health very markedly, and he established the following ratio of mortality for the different regions: The ratio for mountains and elevated regions he observed to be one in thirty-eight; on the banks of rivers, one in twenty-six; on the level plains, sown with grain, one in twenty-four, and in parts interspersed with pools and marshes, one in twenty.

VI.

The influence and value of pure and healthy air may be seen in the simplest physiological observations.

Animal life is fed and sustained by respiration, as well as vegetable life. It is from the blood that animal life derives the materials and forces which maintain it, and we have seen how this owes its vivifying properties, in a great measure, to the oxygen which it receives from the respiratory organs, and how its power is in direct ratio to the purity of the air breathed. A vitiated atmosphere manifests itself at once in the nutritive powers of the vital stream; and the more feeble the respiration, the less rich the blood. This " oxygen enters by the lungs into the blood, and with the blood flows on and circulates through the body; it also enters partly into the composition of the tissues, so that it is a real food, and it is as necessary to the construction of the human body as the other forms of food which are usually introduced into the stomach."

The weight of oxygen, says Professor Johnston, taken up by the lungs, exceeds considerably that of all the dry, solid food which is introduced into the stomach of a healthy man.

Man consumes one hundred gallons of air every hour, ordinarily with eighteen respirations per minute, and two hundred and six cubic feet of air is the minimum for the preservation of health. The minimum allowed to the English hospitals by artificial ventilation is twenty-two hundred cubic feet the hour. The patients of St. Guy's receive four thousand cubic feet of fresh air every hour. The quantity required by the sick is enormous, to compensate the products of respiration, and all the deleterious evaporations of the locality where they are placed, and all other effluvia of diverse natures. In the Hospital Lariboissaire, at Paris, where about fifteen hundred cubic feet of air are furnished by machinery every hour, a taint is perceptible in the atmosphere: and Morin, in his experiments at Hospital Beaujon, thought that two thousand cubic feet were hardly sufficient. Dr. Sutherland believes four thousand feet to be necessary. The quantity, however, is nothing compared to quality. The quality is of the highest importance. The air must contain the vivifying properties of its normal constitution, or it loses force, and death must ensue. The source of animal heat is in the mutual chemical action of the oxygen and the constituents of the blood conveyed by the circulation. When the atmosphere is impure the oxidating processes are much diminished. We receive into our lungs about one hundred gallons of air per hour, and from this we absorb about five gallons of oxygen, or about one twentieth of the volume of air inspired.

" The essential and fundamental condition of all respiration is the reciprocal action of the nourishing fluid, and a medium containing oxygen." Dumas believes that oxygen is necessary to the conservation of the vitality and proper structure of the globules of the blood; also that the integrity of these organisms is one of the essential conditions to the arterialization of the nourishing stream.

Milne Edwards, also, maintains that the great absorbing powers of the blood exist in the globules. The normal number of these globules is one hundred and twenty-seven out of the thousand component parts of the blood; but they vary according to the barometer of health; sometimes they are observed in disease to descend to sixty-five. Vierodt has shown how a certain limit in the number of blood globules in the mammalia cannot be passed in the descending scale without death taking place. Simon and others have also shown how a careful and nutritious regimen may increase these globules in the blood of the consumptive, bringing them up from sixty-four to even one hundred and forty-four.

The blood of man is the richest of all the mammalia, and it contains, according to Berzelius, three times as many hydrochlorates as the blood of the ox.

Its richness depends upon the species and individual, and also upon the degree of health, it varying according to the condition of the person.

" A diseased pathological condition causes a diminution in the proportion of active principles of the nourishing fluid, and especially in fibrine, of which the abundance is allied to the most important activity of the vital work in some parts of the organism." " The blood," says Dr. Jones, " is not only distributed by innumerable channels through every recess of the body; the blood is not only the source of all the elements of structure; the blood not only furnishes the materials for all the secretions and excretions, and for all the chemical changes,—but the blood is in turn affected by the physical and chemical changes of every vessel, of every nerve, of every organ and texture of the body. It is evident then that the constitution of the blood will depend upon the food, upon the vigor and perfection of the organs of digestion, respiration, circulation, secretion, and excretion; upon the vigor and perfection of the nervous system, and of all the organs and apparatus; and upon the correlation of the physical, vital, and nervous forces. The character of the blood will then vary with the animal; with the organ and tissue through which it is circulating; with the age, sex, temperament, race, diet, previous habits, occupation, and previous diseases; with the soil and climate; and with the relative states of the activity of the forces."

VII.

Thus it appears how important is the function of respiration, and how vital the necessity for pure air.

Pure dry air contains about 21 gallons of oxygen, and 79 gallons of nitrogen out of 100, and about one gallon of carbonic acid out of 2500. Man will consume, on the average of 20 respirations a minute, or 1200 respirations the hour, about 20 pounds of air, and give off $2\frac{1}{2}$ pounds or more of carbonic acid, besides half a pound of watery vapor, per diem, or, according to Andral and Gavaret, 22 quarts of carbonic acid per hour. We have shown in the chapter on Alimentation how this process of respiration affects the nutrition, and how serious the results of its disturbance. The purer the air, the more perfect the type of men and animals. This was understood by the ancients, and they established their most famous schools for gladiatorial training at Capua and Ravenna.

6

The same law is observed at the present day by the admirers of the race-horse. The purity of the air gives purity to the blood, and the blood builds up the system in like proportion of excellence.

VIII.

Fifteen hundred cubic inches, or twenty-two quarts, of carbonic acid are expired from the lungs every hour, and thrown off into the surrounding atmosphere. Besides this, Sequin found that 18 grains of organized matter were thrown off per minute from the body in the form of insensible perspiration, — 7 grains by the lungs, and 11 grains by the skin. Hence we may form some idea of the rapid corruption of the air in this stockade, where 30,000 men were breathing at one time. The foul and heavy vapors could not rise above the palisades unless a strong breeze prevailed ; and even then they became so offensive as almost to extinguish life, like the deadly air of the Grotta del Cane. The exhalations from putrescent animal surfaces are always specifically heavier than the upper warm strata in the confined spaces where men are crowded together, such as the wards of hospitals. We find, according to Professor Graham, the vitiated air to be composed somewhat as follows : Phosphoretted hydrogen, sulphuretted hydrogen, carbonic acid, carburetted hydrogen, cyanogen with its compounds. The first gas is always recognized where the diseases of the internal organs are present, especially affections of the liver, stomach, bowels, and in fever and dysentery ; and we observe the blackening of the lead plaster, &c., when the second is present. Stupor, headache, and sleepiness betray the presence of the other three gases. The diffusion of each gas is always inversely as the square root of the density of such gases.

The density is thus, air being regarded as 1000 : —

Phosphuretted hydrogen, ... 1240
Sulphuretted " 1170
Carburetted " 559
Carbonic acid, ... 1524
Cyanogen, ... 1806

IX.

The report of the British Parliament Commission gives the following data in this important question : " The amount of carbonic acid in the air is about $\frac{1}{2000}$, or .0005 ; the amount expired is about $\frac{1}{12}$, or .083. Respired air contains $\frac{1}{10}$ or 1 of carbonic acid, and this must be diluted ten times to make the air safe. Thus, $\frac{1}{10} \div \frac{10}{1} = \frac{1}{100}$, or .01 ; and this again divided by 10, or $\frac{1}{100} \div \frac{10}{1} = \frac{1}{1000}$, or .001, gives the amount of ventilation needed to reduce the air to that state of purity that only $\frac{1}{1000}$ more of carbonic acid should be added to the air, when it would be represented by .0015 instead of .0005."

Observing this rule, and taking 300 cubic feet as the air respired for the 24 hours, to dilute it ten times it must be mixed with ten times the bulk, or 3000 cubic feet — the space to be allowed for each individual; but if it is wished to keep up a pure air, it must be mixed with ten times this bulk again, or 30,000 cubic feet, which shows the ventilation needed to maintain an atmosphere nearly pure; or there must be admitted into the space of 3000 cubic feet nearly 21 cubic feet per minute of fresh air by ventilation, if the man in it is to breathe an atmosphere which shall contain only three times more of carbonic acid than the air he breathes originally contained; or again, 300 cubic feet, 3000, and 30,000, mark the requirements of one individual, in 24 hours, for respiration, space, and ventilation. On a calm day, when there were no strong breezes to change the air of the stockade, the entire quantity of air in the old stockade, allowing the palisades to be on the average 20 feet high, could be exhausted in 20 minutes by the 30,000 men respiring 300 cubic inches per minute. This is not a proper estimate to offer; but it will give a just idea of the rapid and fearful vitiation of the air that took place within the enclosure.

Vierodt shows how rapidly carbonic acid increases when foul air is breathed, and Lehman proves the rapid disengagement of the gas in moist atmospheres.

Symptoms of uneasiness manifest themselves when the air contains from $\frac{6}{1000}$ to $\frac{7}{1000}$ of carbonic acid, and when the proportion amounts to ten parts to 100 of air, death ensues. "This effect is visible upon vegetables also, and many of them are extremely susceptible of impurities in the air, and very slight modifications in the proportion of its constituents are more or less prejudicial to their growth." But plants, like animals, vary in regard to the delicacy of their constitutions, some being much more susceptible than others.

In warm climes the respiration becomes slower, and in

consequence there is less of carbon burned and less oxygen absorbed; but on the other hand the functions of the skin become vastly increased, the bilious secretions become more active, and the excess of carbon is eliminated by this channel.

That we expire more carbonic acid in a warm, moist atmosphere, and less in a cold, dry climate, is shown by the exhilaration of our spirits on a fine frosty morning.

No wonder that men lost their reason in this prison, for the blood no longer reddened from the imperfect arterialization, and burdened the brain with its effete matter, paralyzing and clogging up the delicate filaments and the narrow channels of thought and life.

We have seen that the blood is subject to incessant variations in its precise chemical constitution; a free atmosphere, well supplied, oxygenates and destroys the numerous impurities that tend to lurk in the system and develop disease.

Bichat shows, in his researches on life and death, how the black and carbonized blood disturbs the functions of the brain and acts like a narcotic poison, causing the heart finally to cease its throbbings.

These miasms and poisons floated about the enclosure where there was not the least sign of vegetable organism to absorb and convert them. As they passed into the systems of the prisoners they became the cause of disease, decrepitude, and death.

X.

Vitiated air is one of the most subtile and powerful of poisons, and it seems to affect soldiers more than any other class of persons, and its consequences have been commented upon by most of the military writers, — from Xenophon among the Greeks, Vegetius among the Romans, down to those of the present time. Cavalry horses have been observed to suffer deterioration and death from the same cause.

Ague and fever, states Dr. Johnson, " two of the most prominent features of the malarious influences, are as a drop of water in the ocean when compared with the other, but less obtrusive, but more dangerous maladies that silently disorganize the vital structure of the human fabric under the influence of this deleterious and invisible poison."

One fourth of the sailors of the English navy are sent home invalided every year, and one tenth of them die from the effects of foul air of their cabins. " Two thirds of the pulmonary diseases which desolate England are induced by this cause." Baudelocque long ago pointed out its influences in the etiology of scrofula.

It is really the same influence observed by Magendie, and not contradicted to the present day, that putrid blood, brain, bile, or pus, when laid on flesh wounds, produce in animals, after a longer or shorter interval, vomiting, languor, and death. The same results and phenomena are observed in the inspiration of bad air; the most terrible forms of fever arise from the overcrowding of people in confined and limited spaces. Most of the zymotic diseases enter by the lungs, which are the principal absorbing agents.

The breathing in of foul air, loaded with perceptible and putrid animal and vegetable emanations, gives rise to those zymotici, the ideas of which originated with Hippocrates, and to which the distinguished Liebig has since given form and prominence.

Not only is animal life disturbed and destroyed, but we observe that vegetables even are affected by the same or similar causes; that they are extremely susceptible of impurities in the air, and that the rapidity and vigorous appearance of their growth are affected whenever there is very slight modification in the healthy proportions of the atmosphere. Again, we see how seeds, when placed in elementary oxygen, germinate with extreme rapidity, and soon decay, thus indicating how the presence of nitrogen in the natural air restrains the force of the other element.

XI.

There was another serious defect in the management of the prison, and that was, the neglect to provide the means for entire ablution, which, in warm climes, becomes an imperative necessity. "Animals perspire, that they may live;" and this function is as necessary to a healthy life as either breathing or digestion: the skin, like the lungs, gives off carbonic acid and absorbs oxygen. But it differs from the lungs in giving off a much larger bulk of the former gas than it absorbs of the latter. The quantity of carbonic acid which escapes varies with circumstances. It is sometimes equal to one thirtieth, and sometimes amounts to only a ninetieth part of that which is thrown off from the lungs, but generally it amounts to 100 grains daily. But exercise and hard labor increase the evolution of carbon from the skin, as it does from the lungs. A large quantity of nitrogen also escapes by the skin.

Hence we may infer the effect upon the prisoners, from the want of ablution, and the means of removing the accumulating filth of their bodies. The functions of the skin, and their influence in the practical feeding of animals, have been carefully studied by the experimentalists, and they have observed that the difference in washed and unwashed animals, during the process of fattening, amounts to one fifth.

Pure air and the enforcement of daily ablutions having been introduced into some of the English schools, the sick rate was reduced two thirds. A general of a beleaguered city in Spain was obliged to put his soldiers on short allowance, and compelled them to bathe daily in order to amuse them, when he found, to his surprise, that they became in better condition than when on full rations.

Chadwick states, in his papers on Economy, that "amongst soldiers of the line who have only hands and face washing provided for, the death-rate is upwards of 17 per 1000."

When sent into prisons where there is a far lower diet, sometimes exclusively vegetable, and without beer or spirits, but where regular head to foot ablutions and cleanliness of clothes, as well as of persons, are enforced, their health is vastly increased, and the death-rate is reduced to $2\frac{1}{2}$ per 1000.

XII.

It appears from the mortuary records of the prison that 13,000 men were registered and buried during the year of its occupation. It also appears from the same hospital lists that 17,873 men received medical treatment, or were known to be sick, and their names entered in the books. Of these, 825 men were exchanged, leaving 17,048 to be accounted for; thus giving a mortality of more than 76 per cent., or 760 men out of every thousand.

It is said, and stated with confidence, that the names of the 4000 soldiers who died in their mud-holes within the pen, and who did not generally receive any medical treatment whatever, were placed upon the hospital register, and their diseases diagnosed after death and removal from the stockade. But of this the writer is not positive, although he has seen tables of statistics of certain periods of the prison, where it is shown that every patient who was treated for disease perished.

XIII.

To form an idea of the awful mortality which reigned here, let us review the records of the hospital prisons, and the casualties of armies of foreign as well as our own country. These comparisons must, however, be received with much allowance, for the circumstances which led to death are very different.

* * * * *

In the prisons of Switzerland, before they were im-

6 *

proved, the mortality was 25 to 35 per 1000. In the county jails of England it is reckoned at 10 per 1000 ; in the terrible hulks (Les Bagnes) of France it is 39 to 55 per 1000, including epidemics of cholera.

The average mortality of the London hospitals, where only the severer cases of disease and accident are received and treated, is nine per cent.

In the hospitals of Dublin it is less than 5 per cent. ; in the civil hospitals of France it is from 5 to 9 per cent. ; in the military hospitals of the same country it is much less ; at Val de Grace it was 4 per cent. for a period of forty years ; at Vincennes it was 2 per cent. for a long period ; at the Gros Caillou, for a term of eleven years, it was less than 3 per cent. out of 55,000 patients.

The mortality at Moyamensing Prison for many years was 1 per cent., and in the New York Penitentiary less than that for seven years. The average deaths in the prisons of Massachusetts, Michigan, New York, and Maryland, was about 2 per cent. The death-rate of the rebels con-fined in our military prisons was small, comparatively : at Fort Delaware it was 2 per cent. for eleven months ; at Johnson's Island it was 2 per cent., or 134 deaths out of 6000 prisoners, for the period of twenty-one months.

The loss at the rebel prison at Elmira is not known for the entire term ; but it was much less than the rebel " Vinculis " desires to make it.

His own statements make but 4 per cent. during the worst month for instance : " Now out of less than nine thousand five hundred prisoners on the first of Septem-ber, 386 died that month."

"At Andersonville the mortality averaged 1000 per month

out of 36,000 prisoners, or $\frac{1}{36}$. At Elmira it was 386 per month, out of 9500, or $\frac{1}{25}$ of the whole. At Elmira it was 4 per cent.; at Andersonville less than 3 per cent.

" If the mortality at Andersonville had been as great as at Elmira, the deaths should have been fourteen hundred and forty per month, or fifty per cent. more than they were."

The official records of Andersonville show that Vinculis is greatly in error; for, instead of fourteen hundred and forty, the great number he imagines, they were even more ; for the figures show two thousand six hundred and seventy-eight for September, or more than fifteen per cent., and in October fifteen hundred and ninety-five, or more than twenty-seven per cent., and in the month of August three thousand men died, and on the twenty-third of that month one hundred and twenty-seven perished, or one every eleven minutes out of the number present.

XIV.

In the hospitals of the allied forces, during the campaign of the Crimea, which were established along the banks of the Bosphorus and at Constantinople, there were admitted, during the twenty-two months of the war, one hundred and thirty-nine thousand patients, and of these nineteen per cent. were lost during the entire period, or at the rate of ten per cent. per annum.

One hundred and ninety-three thousand patients were admitted into the French hospitals during the same period, and but fourteen per cent. were lost, or less than eight per cent. per annum.

The mortality of the military hospitals of the army of occupation of Spain in 1824 was less than five per cent.

The extemporized and regular hospitals of Milan, says Baron Larrey, received during the Italian campaign thirty-four thousand sick and wounded; of whom fourteen hundred died, or four per cent., or forty men out of every one thousand. The temporary hospitals of Nashville received during the year 1864 sixty-five thousand sick and wounded, of whom twenty-six hundred died, or four per cent. The numerous hospitals of Washington treated in 1863 sixty-eight thousand patients, and lost twenty-six hundred, or less than four per cent.; and, in 1864, the same hospitals treated ninety-six thousand patients (forty-nine thousand sick and forty-seven thousand wounded), and lost six thousand, or six per cent. The department of Pennsylvania received fifty-six thousand patients in its various hospitals, and lost but two per cent. Twenty-nine thousand nine hundred patients were cared for in the medical and surgical wards of the fourteen great civil hospitals of London in 1861, and but twenty-seven hundred of these died, or nine per cent. The diary of the rebel War Clerk says, that in the hospitals of the rebel service sixteen hundred thousand patients were treated, with a loss of four per cent.; yet it appears from a surreptitious copy of the quarterly report ending 1864, relating to the prisoners in hospital at Richmond, that twenty-seven hundred patients were treated, and thirteen hundred and ninety-six died, or fifty per cent.; more than half of these cases were those of diarrhœa and dysentery, and only seventy deaths from fever. It appears from the official data of the Surgeon-

General's office, published in November, 1865, that eight hundred and seventy thousand cases of wounds and disease were treated by the medical staff of the United States army in 1862, and but two per cent. were lost; also, that in 1863, seventeen hundred thousand cases were cared for, with a loss of three per cent. only.

XV.

The statistics of the great armies of Austria, Sardinia, and France during the Italian war, when half a million of men met in conflict at Magenta and Solferino, show, according to Boudin, that but six thousand four hundred and ten men lost their lives — of the French, three thousand five hundred and five; of the Sardinians, one thousand and forty-five; of the Austrians, one thousand eight hundred and sixty. It is shown by the records of the British army, that, out of the aggregate number of four hundred and thirty-eight thousand British soldiers who were engaged in the twenty-two great battles of the British empire from 1801 to 1854, but fourteen thousand men were killed, or died of their wounds, or three per cent. These battles embrace those of Egypt, Spain, France, Waterloo, and the Crimea.

Contrast these blood-stained records with this one instance of rebel cruelty at Andersonville. Of the number of the Federal soldiers who have been held in captivity during the rebellion by the rebels, more than thirty thousand of them are now dead. We know from official records that twenty-three thousand are buried at Andersonville and Salisbury alone.

XVI.

Up to the month of September, 1864, forty-two thousand four hundred prisoners had been received, and out of this number seven thousand five hundred and eighty-seven, or eighteen per cent., had died since the occupation of the prison — a period of about six months. During August the manœuvres of Sherman alarmed them so much that they thought best to remove many of the prisoners to other stockades in Alabama and in North and South Carolina; but yet the mortality for the remainder of the year was for the month of September seventeen per cent. out of the number present; October, twenty-seven per cent.; November, twenty-four per cent.; and seven per cent. in December, when there were but five thousand inmates. This gives nineteen per cent. average for each of those four months, and indicates that out of the thirty-two thousand present on the first of August, but few thousand would have been living at the close of the year, had not Sherman compelled a reduction in the number of inmates. Out of this number present in August, and distributed afterwards, I believe that but few thousand survived the system of treatment at the other prisons, and ever lived to reach home. Of these few thousand men who were finally exchanged, a great many have since perished; which statement will be admitted by all who have watched the phases of disease since the termination of the war.

XVII.

The records' state that eight thousand died from diarrhœa and scurvy, and that three thousand more died from dysentery and unknown causes. Two hundred and fifteen thousand cases of diarrhœa were treated in the United States army in 1862, and but one thousand one hundred died; and of thirty-seven thousand cases of dysentery, but three hundred and forty-seven died; and but one death from scurvy per thirty-five thousand of mean strength. In 1863, according to the official records by Surgeon Woodward, five hundred thousand cases of diarrhœa and dysentery were treated, and but two per cent. died. According to the same authority there were but eight thousand six hundred cases of scurvy during the first two years of the war, and but one per cent. of these died. Fever was almost unknown, although the foul atmospheres and malarial miasms are generally so eager in their attacks, and so rapid in their effects; the autopsies of the dead men revealed to the astonished pathologist the utter absence of all the usual lesions of these diseases.

Boudin, of the French army, in 1843, in his " Essai de Geographie Medicale," observes that phthisis and typhoid fever are very rare in the marshy districts where intermittent fevers of a certain gravity prevail. It does not appear that either of these diseases declared itself to any perceptible degree.

The effect of starvation was so strong that miasmatic disease could not gain a lodgment in the system, although every other condition was favorable to its production. Scurvy seems to be prominent in the alleged diseases.

The combined influence of all the vicious conditions could readily have produced this form of malady in its worst shape; but it is one of those diseases which are clearly within the control of man, and for the existence of which, in this case, there is no excuse whatever. They required the treatment, practised with success in India, for those fluxes which are marked by a scorbutic state of the system — potatoes and lime juice.

The neighboring plantations produced the potatoes in great quantities. In the everglades of Florida the lime tree, which furnishes a positive antidote, grows in wild luxuriance; and the woods everywhere, the corn and potatoes of their fields, furnish vinegar by distillation. If the plantations failed in their supplies of vegetables, the forests furnished, with trifling labor, an excellent substitute.

Vinegar, in the early history of war, was the chief and the sure reliance against the attacks of scurvy and malaria. To this drink chiefly, Marshal Saxe ascribes the amazing success of the Roman campaigns in the varied climates of Europe, Asia, and Africa. Scientific men, from Dioscorides to Orfila, have extolled its virtues in this respect. It is idle to say that they did not know how to make it, for the merest tyro in chemistry understands the method of fermentation and distillation.

XVIII.

It has been stated that the mortality was caused by epidemics; by dysentery or camp distempers; but the testimony of nature, as revealed by the scalpel of the dissector, does not admit of such statement. There was neither epidemic nor pestilence. There was starvation instead.

That a vast amount of this mortality was caused by the unfavorable, the needless, the cruel circumstances in which the prisoners were placed, no one acquainted with the phenomena of life and death will deny.

But as to how much more than the normal rate, no man has sufficient generosity and impartiality to determine.

This we know, however, that it is an axiom with all hygienists and military men, that the health of the soldier is always in direct ratio of the care taken of him. To give a just estimate of the normal degree of the mortality that was caused by diarrhœa, will indeed form a complex problem, since it is not only the last stage of starvation, but it is often produced by the decomposition of the blood by the dyscrasia peculiar to camp life. We observe it in all armies during the summer months, and that it seems to result from manifold causes. Although the predisposing cause is the dyscrasiac condition of the soldier, the determining cause is most always the quality of the food consumed, and the purity of the water used for potable purposes. Surface water mixed with confervoids and decomposed vegetable matter, and the deeper currents of water which pass through the rotten limestones, are, during the summer, the fruitful sources of intestinal disorders.

Those who have observed the influence of atmospheric changes upon disease, will comprehend why the diarrhœa curve followed the line of high temperature, and how it progressed in consequence of heat, even when unassisted by inanition.

XIX.

It has been maintained by the rebels that many of the deaths were caused by nostalgia, or home-sickness. The truth of this remark we do not consider of sufficient importance to discuss in the extenuation of the crime, although we will admit that this disorder, which impairs the intellectual faculties and enfeebles the digestive functions, is often the cause of death among the French armies in Algeria, and the English in India, and that it can even become epidemic and lead to suicide. But the disease is clearly within the control of man.

We can find a more ready reason for the explanation of the derangement of the mind and nervous system in the dietary. The statistics of insanity show how sad or ferocious delirium may arise from starvation ; and according to Combe, " a species of insanity, arising from defective nourishment, is very prevalent among the Milanese, and is easily cured by the nourishing diet provided in the hospitals to which the patients are sent."

The survivors have explained the causes of death of their comrades. The faces of these men told the story better than the tongue could describe. The peculiar look of these men was common to them all : the shrunken and pallid features — the rough and blighted skin — the vacant, wild, and unearthly stare of the hollow and lustreless eye, — all told of the results of starvation. This look can no more be described than forgotten, when once seen. Wherever the returned sufferers landed, the bystanders were struck with horror by this fearful appearance.

XX.

The impure air, the marked and rapid changes of temperature, and the foul water, rendered the tenacity of animal life a simple problem, and when joined to the deprivation of food, it became a matter of surprise that any of the hapless wretches escaped with life.

The intense heat served to accelerate the destruction of the organism, already weakened and sapped by the want of food and the putridity of the atmosphere.

Life is always best supported at a moderate temperature, which, however, is restricted to a certain degree, depending upon the forces of reserve in the animal; and it is observed by experimentalists that all the vital properties of the nervous centres, the nerves and muscles in adult as well as in young warm-blooded animals, may be much increased by a diminution of temperature.

This is shown by Brown-Sequard, in his illustrations of the influences of prolonged muscular exertion on cadaveric rigidity and putrefaction.

Some few of the soldiers arriving from the army, with their systems already saturated with paludal and animal poisons, and who were profoundly cachectic, could rally very slowly if at all, under the combined influences of the mephitic miasms and heat of the locality, even had there been no fault in the alimentation. But there was a very great number of the prisoners who were free from disease and debility, as they were direct from their homes in the North, or from the healthy camps of instruction.

Scurvy and the vicious forms of zymotic disease, which depend upon starvation and vitiated atmosphere, raged unchecked. The medical care does not seem to have made any impression upon them, because of the limitations of their materia medica, and the want of attention and accommodations for the patients.

There does not seem to have been any sanitary regulations, nor the simplest hygienic precautions adopted by the prison authorities. No proper military arrangements to enforce order among the turbulent or insane, to protect the weak from the strong in the struggle for a morsel of bread, a bone, or a rag of clothing; no proper system of nurses to assist the feeble within the stockade or the hospital, and administer to their wants. Filth was deposited everywhere, because the enfeebled and dying wretches had not sufficient strength to crawl down to the quagmire by the banks of the stream. In the midst of these horrible circumstances, men met their fate with singular calmness and stoicism. Nature strangely appears to conform and temper the asperities of fate to men and animals alike.

XXI.

It is often asked why the prisoners did not revolt, and with the mighty energy of despair wrench down the gates, and strangle with their hands the few thousand of rebel guards. To burst through the massive timbers of the gates and the outer lines of palisades, and then force the encircling row of ramparts, which were bristling with troops and cannon, required something more than courage. This gigantic strength, this desperation of vigor, was not possible for the prisoners; for the food, and the external impressions — whether of the heat, cold, or horror — had too much impoverished the blood, — the blood, which imparts force to human volition.

XXII.

In the summing up of the condition to which life was exposed in this stockade, and reviewing the vicious influences at work, we may come to some definite conclusion as to the true causes of the results. It is evident from the comparisons and estimates of the dietary that the want of food alone was sufficient to cause a great number of deaths. It is also evident from the statements relative to ratio of density, to exposure, to deadly miasms, and exhalations from decomposing animal matter, that these conditions were alone sufficient to cause excessive mortality, even if the alimentation had been generous and proper.

This terrible mortality, without the influence of epidemics, is without parallel, and is without excuse, save on the principle that war is for mutual destruction, that the captor has the right of disposal, and that the captives must be put to death. The philanthropist may console himself with the idea that climate, with its unseen but powerful agencies, has been the author of the destruction of this army of men; but the surgeon and man of science will recognize the true causes, and express their opinion in but one word, and that word is MURDER : that it was deliberate destruction; but whether with the conscience of the Tartar, or with premeditated free-will, it matters little, — the result is the same.

BOOK SEVENTH.

I.

W AR," exclaims the author of the " Social Contract," " is not exactly a relation of man to man, but a relation of state to state, in which the individuals are enemies only by accident, and not as men, neither even as citizens, but as soldiers, — not exactly as members of the country, but as its defenders. In fine, every state can have as enemies only other states, and not men, on account of the interference of things of diverse natures, which cannot fix any true relation.

" This principle is even conformed to maxims established in all times, and to the constant practice of all civilized people. The declarations of war are more as warnings to the powers than to their subjects. The stranger — either king, or individual, or people — who seizes, kills, or detains the subjects, without declaring the war to the ruler, is not an enemy, he is a brigand.

" Even in open war, a just ruler seizes property in an

enemy's country, all that which belongs to the public; but he respects the person and the property of the individual; he respects the rights upon which his own are founded.

"The intent of the war being the destruction of the hostile state, we have the right to kill the defenders so often as they have arms in their hands; but as soon as they lay them down, and surrender, ceasing to be enemies, or instruments of the enemy, they become again simply men, and we have no longer a right to their lives. Sometimes we may destroy a state without killing a single one of its members; but war does not confer any right which is not necessary to its end.

"These principles are not those of Grotius: they are not founded upon the authorities of poets: but they are derived from the nature of things, and are founded upon reason. With regard to the right of conquest, it has no other foundation than the law of the most force. If war does not give to the conqueror the right to massacre the vanquished people, that right, which he has not, does not establish that to enslave. We have no more right to kill an enemy than to make him a slave. The right to enslave does not then come from the right to kill. This is then an unjust exchange, to compel him to purchase life at the price of liberty, upon which we have no right.

"In establishing the right of life and death upon the right of slavery, and the right to enslave upon the right of life and death, is it not clear that we fall into a wicked circle?"

II.

Says Mirabeau, in his beautiful essay on "Despotism," "We can destroy the life of a man for a frightful crime; but that is not to appropriate my existence when it is forced from me. Consider, upon this subject, how absurd is the opinion of the pretended philosophers who have established force as title; who have set up a right of conquest, and recognized to the conquerors the legitimate power to grant life or put to death.

"It is not true that the right of life and death, exercised by a man upon another man, has ever been anything else than an act of frenzy; for your enemy reduced to slavery can be yet useful to you, provided you preserve his life, — and this is less than the right that he has upon you, and the relation which binds you together; but the massacre of a man is nothing more than to dishonor and disgust humanity, * * * the right of life and death, * * * and what other has the Creator to exercise over our existence?

"From man to man the rights then are always respective. Personal propriety cannot surrender itself, liberty cannot alienate itself. This first gift of nature is imprescriptible; and men, even in their delirium, cannot renounce it."

III.

"Opinion makes the law." If human laws are uncertain and contradictory, it is not the fault of nature, since man has invented or discovered rules in the science of physics which are constant and invariable, like those of geometry and chemistry.

Whatever renders the laws of society invariable, inoperative, is due to the inherent weakness of their basis, and not to the eternal principles of truth and justice. All human laws must be founded on that fundamental and immutable law of nature, "Whatsoever ye would that men should do to you, do ye even so to them." This precept of divine origin is the great balance of the human mind; and it is the secret spring of the progress of nations, as well as the social development of individuals: for without this principle the world would be nothing but a vast arena, in which all classes of people would be arrayed against each other in deadly conflict; impelled by the force of passion and appetite, error and prejudice would soon banish the influence of truth and reason. The weaker families would soon be consumed by the stronger in the wars of avarice and religion.

"The laws of nature," writes M. Regis, "are the dictates of right reason, which teach every man how he is to use his natural right; and the laws of nations are the dictates, in like manner, of right reason, which teach every state how to act and behave themselves toward others."

"As God," says Blackstone, "when he created matter, and endowed it with a principle of mobility, established certain rules for the perpetual direction of that motion, so when he created man, and endued him with free will to conduct himself in all parts of life, he laid down certain immutable laws of human nature whereby that free will is in some degree regulated and restrained, and gave him also the faculty of reason to discover the purport of those laws."

This law of nature being coeval with mankind, and

7

dictated by God himself, is of course superior in obligation to any other. It is binding all over the globe, in all countries and at all times: no human laws are of any validity if contrary to this; and such of them as are valid, derive all their force and all their authority, mediately or immediately, from this original.

Human laws originate in the wisdom of man, and are designed to regulate their behavior to one another, and are enforced by human authority and worldly sanctions.

The fear of punishment and revenge are not strong enough to control the lusts and passions of men.

The true idea and comprehension of the majesty and mercy of the law is infused by the spirit of philosophy.

IV.

" The existence of states," says Montesquieu, " is like that of man, and the first have the right to make war for their proper preservation ; the latter have the right to kill in the case of natural defence. In the case of natural defence I have the right to kill, since my life is my own, as the life of him who attacks me belongs to himself. * * * From the right of war follows that of conquest, which is the consequence : it ought then to follow the spirit. * * * It is clear when the conquest is made, the conqueror has no longer the right to kill, since he is no longer in the position of natural defence, or for his proper preservation.

" That which has made them think thus (right to kill), is that they have believed that the conqueror had the right to destroy society, whence they have concluded that they had that to destroy the men who composed it, which is a false consequence extracted from a false principle. Because the society should perish, it does not follow that the men who form it ought also to perish. Society is a union of men, and not men: the citizen can perish and the man remain. From the right to kill in conquest, politics have derived the right to enslave; but the consequence is as badly founded as the principle."

There are certain rules that arise from the principle of self-preservation, and form what Wolff calls " the voluntary law of nations." " Hence it follows that all nations have a right to repel by force what openly violates the law of the society which nature has established among them, or that directly attacks the welfare and safety of that society. At the same time care must be taken not to extend this law to the prejudice of the liberty of nations."

v.

The right of jurisdiction belongs only to those societies which have united for the purpose of maintaining the natural rights of each individual.

The ablest writers have maintained that society has not the right of life and death, and whoever arrogates that power commits a " divine *lèse majesté*." " The object, the interest, and the function of all government are, then, to maintain the harmony of society established upon the moral relations of justice, and upon the physical order that no human power can change, and to protect all those who compose that society." Louis XI., that Tiberius of France, caused to be put to death more than four thousand persons, and nearly all without process of law.

We see passionate men defending palpable errors with fanaticism and metaphysical temerity, as though they were divine dogmas. Thus Slavery would legalize frightful tyranny, and declare permanent proscriptions, with the same ease that it consigned thousands to starvation. " If liberty," says the author of the " Essai sur le Despotisme," " is the first of resorts for man, Slavery must alter all the sentiments, blunt all the sensations, and denaturalize them ; stifle all talent, blend all shades, corrupt all the orders of state, and scatter discord, the germ of anarchy and revolutions. Man is only wicked when a superstitious institution or a tyrannical government gives the example of ferocity, and supplies him with fear for motive and cupidity for passion. But it is necessary to distinguish with men the character acquired from natural inclination : we are, of all beings, the most susceptible of modifications, and above all, of extreme passions. An enslaved people are always vile : they can be wicked and cruel, because they are irritable, gloomy, and ignorant; and when, although instruction will not be the only rampart of liberty against tyranny, it will always be the first safeguard of man against man ; but the slave is a mutilated man."

Every writer will admit this whose pen is not enslaved by fear, or rendered venal by interest.

VI.

The right of making prisoners of war, and depriving them of their liberty, and of the power and opportunity of farther resistance, is undoubted, for it is founded on the principles of security and self-defence. But when the soldier has laid down his arms, and submitted to the will of tne conqueror, the right of taking his life ceases, unless he should forfeit the right himself by some new crime; and the savage errors of antiquity, in putting prisoners to death, have long been renounced by civilized nations.

Among the European states prisoners of war are seldom ill-treated; and when the number of prisoners is so great as not to be fed, or kept with safety, it has been the custom to parole them, either for a certain length of time, or for the war. All authorities agree that they cannot be made slaves, although under certain circumstances they may be set at labor on the public fortifications and works.

Prisoners of war are retained to prevent their returning to the field of conflict, and there are times when they may be detained and refused all ransom, when, for instance, it is obvious that the parole will not be regarded by the opposing commanders, and when their exchange would throw a preponderance of weight into the ranks of the antagonist. It would have been very dangerous for the Czar Peter the Great to have exchanged his Swedish prisoners for an equal number of unequal Russians; but whilst retained they were treated with kindness.

VII.

The rebel policy and system towards the Federal prisoners, along the entire line, without exception, from Virginia to Texas, was one of stupendous atrocity. It was one of the most inhuman and monstrous that hate and tyranny ever invented. It was no less derogatory to human character than defiant to the principles of Christianity; but Christianity was unknown there. The gods of worship were the deities of the dark ages, and the fancied garlands of flowers that decorated their statues were nothing more than wreaths of cyprus leaves. This stockade was the epitome and concentration of all earthly misery, to which the Bastile and the Inquisition offer but feeble comparisons, as prototypes, as models, as ideas, for the destruction of human life.

In this we recognize the perversion of the natural sentiments after two centuries of crime, the defiance of all honorable law, " the barbarism of slavery."

What can we, in extenuation, ascribe to recklessness, what to ignorance? " There is," says the eloquent Rousseau, " a brutal and ferocious ignorance, which springs from a bad heart and a false spirit. A criminal ignorance, which extends itself even to the duties of humanity; which multiplies vices, which degrades reason, debases the soul, and renders man like the beasts."

These men destroyed the strength, the lives of thousands, by stealthy means, and excused their consciences by the reflections of perverted nature: as Timour said to his victims, " It is you who assassinate your own souls!"

VIII.

It has been the custom, among European nations, to treat prisoners of war liberally, and the expenses of maintaining them are paid by both sides at the close of the war.

The British Parliament voted, in 1780, to pay forty thousand pounds sterling to disinfect and improve the prison where the Spanish prisoners were confined, and where a fatal fever had declared itself. And there are many instances where European powers have acted kindly and humanely towards those who had fallen into their power from hazard of battle. War was declared against states, and not against the individual subjects of those states.

At all times, kindness to the unfortunate, and hospitality to strangers, has always been considered as a virtue of the first rank among people whose manners are simple, and who, uncontaminated by vices of a false and frivolous civilization, exhibit the natural qualities of the human race. Even among the darkness of the middle ages kindness was compulsory, and hospitality enforced by statute, and whoever denied succor to misery was liable to punishment. "Quicunque hospiti venienti lectum aut focum negaverit trium solidorum in latione mulctetur." (Leg. Burgund., tit. 38, § 1.)

The laws of the Slavi ordained that the movables of an inhospitable person should be confiscated, and his house burned.

IX.

In comparison with these humane provisions, how terribly contrasted are the modes of treatment as practised by the rebel authorities upon the Federal soldiers! "Let us hoist the black flag, and kill every prisoner," said one of the cabinet officers. "I will sell my wheat," said another cabinet officer, "to my fellow-citizens, at exorbitant prices." "My God," said a poor woman, "how can I pay such prices! I have seven children? What shall I do?" "I do not know, madam," was the brutal answer, "unless you eat them."

When such sentiments prevailed at Richmond, what could be expected in kindness by those who were looked upon with hatred and as worthy of death?

In the revolutionary times of 1776 there was no brutal treatment of prisoners of war by Americans. Washington was extremely solicitous that no act of barbarity should stain the sanctity of the cause. In a letter of May 11, 1776, Washington wrote to the President of Congress, recommending that measures be adopted to secure for prisoners of war the most humane treatment; and again to the Massachusetts Committee, February 6, 1776, he wrote, recommending that captives should be treated with humanity and kindness. The Continental Congress passed a resolution in 1776 that all taken with arms be treated as prisoners of war, but with humanity, and allowed the same rations as the troops in the service of the United States.

X.

The United States Government adopted the following rules in 1863 for the guidance of our armies, and published them in General Order, No. 100, April 24: —

* * * *

11. The law of war not only disclaims all cruelty and bad faith concerning engagements concluded with the enemy during the war, but also the breaking of stipulations solemnly contracted by the belligerents in time of peace, and avowedly intended to remain in force in case of war between the contracting powers.

It disclaims all extortions and other transactions for individual gain ; all acts of private revenge, or connivance at such acts.

Offences to the contrary shall be severely punished, and especially so if committed by officers.

14. Military necessity, as understood by modern civilized nations, consists in the necessity of those measures which are indispensable for securing the ends of war, and which are lawful according to the modern law and usages of war.

15. Military necessity admits of all direct destruction of life or limb of armed enemies, and of other persons whose destruction is incidentally unavoidable in the armed contests of the war ; it allows of the capturing of every armed enemy, and every enemy of importance to the hostile government, or of peculiar danger to the captor ; it allows of all destruction of property, and obstruction of the ways and channels of traffic, travel, or communication, and of all withholding of sustenance

7 *

or means of life from the enemy; of the appropriation of whatever an enemy's country affords necessary for the safety and subsistence of the army, and of such deception as does not involve the breaking of good faith, either positively pledged regarding agreements entered into during the war, or supposed by the modern law of war to exist. Men who take up arms against one another in public war do not cease on this account to be moral beings, responsible to one another and to God.

16. Military necessity does not admit of cruelty, — that is, the infliction of suffering for the sake of suffering or revenge, — nor of maiming or wounding, except in fight, nor of torture to extort confessions. It does not admit of the use of poison in any way, nor of the wanton devastation of a district. It admits of deception, but disdains acts of perfidy; and, in general, military necessity does not include any act of hostility which renders the return to peace unnecessarily difficult.

27. The law of war can no more wholly dispense with retaliation than can the law of nations, of which it is a branch; yet civilized nations acknowledge retaliation as the sternest feature of war. A reckless enemy often leaves to his opponents no other means of securing himself against the repetition of barbarous outrage.

28. Retaliation will, therefore, never be resorted to as a measure of mere revenge, but only as a means of protective retribution, and cautiously and unavoidably; that is to say, retaliation shall only be resorted to after careful inquiry into the real occurrence and the character of the misdeeds that may demand retribution.

33. It is no longer considered lawful — on the contrary

it is held to be a serious breach of the law of war — to force the subjects of the enemy into the service of the victorious government, except the latter should proclaim, after a fair and complete conquest of the hostile country or district, that it is resolved to keep the country, district, or place permanently as its own, and make it a portion of its own country.

49. A prisoner of war is a public enemy, armed or attached to the hostile army for active aid, who has fallen into the hands of the captor, either fighting or wounded, on the field or in the hospital, by individual surrender or by capitulation.

52. No belligerent has the right to declare that he will treat every captured man in arms, of a levy en masse, as a brigand or bandit. * * *

56. A prisoner of war is subject to no punishment for being a public enemy, nor is any revenge wreaked upon him by the intentional infliction of any suffering, or disgrace by cruel imprisonment, want of food, by mutilation, death, or any other barbarity.

57. So soon as a man is armed by a sovereign government, and takes the soldier's oath of fidelity, he is a belligerent; his killing, wounding, or other warlike acts are no individual crime or offence. * * *

67. The law of nations allows every sovereign government to make war upon another sovereign state, and therefore admits of no rules or laws different from those of regular warfare regarding the treatment of prisoners of war, although they may belong to the army of a government which the captor may consider as a wanton and unjust assailant.

The use of poison in any manner, be it to poison wells, or food, or arms, is wholly excluded from modern warfare. He that uses it puts himself out of the pale of the laws and usages of war.

71. Whoever intentionally inflicts additional wounds on an enemy already wholly disabled, or kills such an enemy, or who orders or encourages soldiers to do so, shall suffer death if duly convicted, whether he belongs to the army of the United States, or is an enemy captured after having committed his misdeed.

72. Money and other valuables on the person of a prisoner, such as watches or jewelry, as well as extra clothing, are regarded by the American army as the private property of the prisoners, and the appropriation of such valuables or money is considered dishonorable, and is prohibited.

74. A prisoner of war, being a public enemy, is the prisoner of the government and not of the captor. No ransom can be paid by a prisoner of war to his individual captor or to any officer in command. The government alone releases captives, according to rules prescribed by itself.

75. Prisoners of war are subject to confinement or imprisonment, such as may be deemed necessary on account of safety, but they are to be subjected to no other intentional suffering or indignity. The confinement and mode of treating a prisoner may be varied during his captivity, according to the demands of safety.

76. Prisoners of war shall be fed upon plain and wholesome food whenever practicable, and treated with humanity. They may be required to work for the benefit of the

captor's government, according to their rank and condition.

77. A prisoner of war who escapes, may be shot or otherwise killed in his flight, but neither death nor any other punishment shall be inflicted upon him, simply for his attempt to escape, which the law of war does not consider a crime. Stricter means of security shall be used after an unsuccessful attempt at escape. * * *

109. The exchange of prisoners of war is an act of convenience to both belligerents. If no general cartel has been concluded it cannot be demanded by either of them. No belligerent is obliged to exchange prisoners of war. A cartel is voidable as soon as either party has violated it.

119. Prisoners of war may be released from captivity by exchange and under certain circumstances, also by parole.

120. The term parole designates the pledge of individual good faith and honor to do, or to omit doing, certain acts after he who gives his parole shall have been dismissed wholly or partially from the power of the captor.

121. The pledge of the parole is always an individual but not a private act.

133. No prisoner of war can be forced by the hostile government to parole himself, and no government is obliged to parole prisoners of war, or to parole all captured officers, if it paroles any. As the pledging of the parole is an individual act, so is paroling, on the other hand, an act of choice on the part of the belligerent.

XI.

From the evidence obtained from different sources, and from the results, it may be properly reasoned that there was a secret and fixed intent on the part of the cabal at Richmond to weaken the Federal armies by destroying the prisoners by starvation and exposure.

The open robbery of all the captives, the neglect of the commissariat when there was no excuse, the refusal to remedy atrocious evils, all betray malice and design. That intrepid and humane officer, Colonel Chandler, made complaint of this prison, in his Inspection Report, as early as July 5, 1864, when he uses the following language: "No shelter whatever, nor materials for constructing any, had been provided by the prison authorities, and the ground being entirely bare of trees, none is within reach of the prisoners; nor has it been possible, from the overcrowded state of the enclosure, to arrange the camp with any system. Each man has been permitted to protect himself as best he can, by stretching his blanket, or whatever he may have about him, on such sticks as he can procure. Of other shelter there has been none. There is no medical attendance within the stockade. Many (twenty yesterday) are carted out daily who have died from unknown causes, and whom the medical officers have never seen. The dead are hauled out by the wagon-load, and buried without coffins, their hands, in many instances, being first mutilated with an axe in the removal of any finger-rings they may have. Raw rations have to be issued to a very large portion, who are entirely unprovided with proper utensils, and furnished so limited a supply of fuel they are compelled to dig with their hands in the filthy marsh before mentioned for roots, &c. No soap or clothing have ever been issued. After inquiry, the writer is confident that, with slight exertions, green corn and other anti-scorbutics could readily be obtained. The present hospital arrangements were only intended for the accommodation of ten thousand men, and are totally insufficient, both in character and extent, for the present need, — the number of prisoners being now more than three times as great. The number of cases requiring medical treatment is in an increased ratio. It is impossible to state the number of sick, many dying within the stockade whom the medical officers have never seen or heard of till their remains are brought out for interment."

Later reports were made by this inspector, and they were forwarded to the rebel executive, indorsed by the assistant-secretary of war, Campbell, that this condition was a reproach to the Confederates as a nation. But not the least notice was taken of these startling and heart-rending revelations, in which Winder was denounced as a murderer from the statements made by Winder himself. The wretch and the system of treatment were denounced by Stephens of South Carolina, by Foote of Tennessee; yet no response was obtained from the secretary of war, or from the executive, Davis. When Breckenridge became secretary of war, shortly before the downfall of the rebellion, the brave Chandler demanded that some notice, some action, should be taken on the reports he had submitted months before, or he would resign his commission; for his honor and humanity were involved.

What action was taken, if any there was, is not known to the writer. The thanks of the South, the kind wishes of all who honor the warm and generous impulses of our better nature, are due to the noble Chandler, who had the courage, the temerity, to expose the suffering condition at Andersonville, and to denounce the authors again and again at the peril of his life.

It is known to the writer that Surgeons Bemis and Fluellen, of the rebel army medical staff, inspected the condition of the prison, and protested against the cruel management.

One of the chief medical officers of the rebel army of the South informed the author that the medical men at this prison were without any influence whatever; and although the prison was within his department for a time, he had no more voice or influence in its management than the man in the moon; and that everything relating to the prison was *controlled and devised by the authorities at Richmond.*

The refusal or the neglect of the rebel authorities, to whom these reports were submitted, to take notice of or remedy the exposed evils, is a tacit acknowledgment and approval of the system at work.

XII.

Northrop, the rebel commissary-general, whom Foote denounced in the rebel Congress as a monster, and incompetent, urged the secretary of war, Seddon, to reduce the rations to gruel and bread, in retaliation for alleged abuses to the rebel prisoners in our hands. Seddon de-

clined to do it openly, on account of the technicalities of
the law; but Northrop took the measure quietly into his
own hands, and withheld meat so often and so long from
the prisoners near Richmond as to call forth a yell of
remonstrance from even the inhuman Winder.

When the prisoners at Belle Isle — numbering from
eight to thirteen thousand — were deprived of meat, —
from the incompetency or the wilfulness of the commissary-general, — for a fortnight at a time, the secretary of
war refused to allow compassionate parties to buy cattle
in the neighborhood of the city, and bring them to the
prison, stating that Northrop had informed him that the
prisoners fared as well as the soldiers.

And in pursuance of this diabolical plan of starvation,
orders were given, in December, by the rebel war department, that no more supplies should be received from
the United States for the prisoners, for which no apology
or reason was ever given.

Winder was denounced by members of Congress; but
Davis took no notice, because he was his personal friend.
Seddon took sides with Northrop, and would not allow
Captain Warner to buy cattle for the prisoners around
Richmond, as he offered to do, and relieve their suffer-
ings.

The postmaster-general wanted to kill the prisoners
taken in raiding; and Seddon, the secretary of war,
stated that he was always in favor of fighting under the
black flag.

When Chandler made his report, Cobb was writing
that all was going on well at the prison. Colonel Persons,
who was the first commander, and relieved by Winder,

applied for an injunction against the prison as a nuisance. No compassion, humanity, or decency was observed in the demand for the process: it was simply a nuisance, and dangerous to the health of the surrounding region. No plea was made that thousands were being murdered there.

XIII.

It is known, and proved beyond "cavil of a doubt," that the prisoners were robbed of all articles of value, even hats, coats, blankets, and shoes, and that no attempt was made to restore them, or to supply any deficiency that arose from this rapacious dishonesty.

In striking contrast with this "barbarism of slavery," notice the treatment in our own prisons, where all needful clothing and blankets were issued to the rebel prisoners, whenever their circumstances required it; and during the period of rebellion, a vast quantity of coats, blankets, stockings, shirts, and drawers were supplied by the quartermaster's department. Thirty-five thousand articles of clothing were issued in eight months to the rebel prisoners at Fort Delaware alone. Of the many thousand rebel wounded and sick prisoners in our hands, who have been under the observation of the writer during the war, all, without exception, were treated with kindness, and the wants of all supplied in the same manner as with our men.

In the Dartmoor prison, the British allowed to each of our men a hammock, a blanket, a horse rug, and a bed containing four pounds of flocks; and every eighteen months one woollen cap, one yellow jacket, one pair of pantaloons, and one waistcoat of the same material as allowed to the British army; and also, every nine months, one pair of shoes, and one shirt. The prison was inspected by the chief surgeon of England, and whenever complaint was made by the prisoners, the admiralty sent officers of high rank to investigate the causes of complaint. The officers of the prison hulks in England behaved generally with kindness and humanity to our men, as is shown by the records of the captivity.

But even this treatment, humane as it appears when compared with the rebel system, was less generous than that bestowed by the Algerine pirates upon our sailors captured by them. The captives in Algiers received good and abundant vegetable food, and were lodged in airy places.

XIV.

This system of barbarity of the rebels towards their prisoners having become known to the United States government, efforts were made to ameliorate the condition of the suffering men, but without avail.

Measures of retaliation were entertained by Congress, in hopes of effecting a change by the clamors from the rebel prisoners themselves, and the following resolutions were introduced by Mr. Wade, of Ohio, but they were not adopted : —

JOINT RESOLUTION, advising Retaliation for the Cruel Treatment of Prisoners by the Insurgents.

Whereas, It has come to the knowledge of Congress that great numbers of our soldiers, who have fallen as prisoners of war into the hands of the insurgents, have been subjected to treatment unexampled for cruelty in the history of civilized war, and finding its parallels only in the conduct of savage tribes; a treatment resulting in the death of multitudes by the slow but designed process of starvation, and by mortal diseases occasioned by insufficient and unhealthy food, by wanton exposure of their persons to the inclemency of the weather, and by deliberate assassination of unoffending men; and the murder, in cold blood, of prisoners after surrender; and, whereas a continuance of these barbarities, in contempt of the laws of war, and in disregard of the remonstrances of the national authorities, has presented to us the alternative of suffering our brave soldiers thus to be destroyed, or to apply the principle of retaliation for their protection: Therefore,

Resolved, by the Senate and House of Representatives of the United States of America, in Congress assembled, That, in the judgment of Congress, it has become justifiable and necessary that the President should, in order to prevent the continuance and recurrence of such barbarities, and to insure the observance by the insurgents of the laws of civilized war, resort at once to measures of retaliation. That, in our opinion, such retaliation ought to be inflicted upon the insurgent officers now in our hands, or hereafter to fall into our hands, as prisoners; that such officers ought to be subjected to like treatment practised towards our officers or soldiers in the hands of the insurgents, in respect to quantity and quality of food, clothing, fuel, medicine, medical attendance, personal exposure, or other mode of dealing with them; that, with a view to the same ends, the insurgent prisoners in our hands ought to be placed under the control and in the keeping of officers and men who have themselves been prisoners in the hands of the insurgents, and have thus acquired a knowledge of their mode of treating Union prisoners; that explicit instructions ought to be given to the forces having the charge of such insurgent prisoners, requiring them to carry out strictly and promptly the principles of this resolution in every case, until the President, having received satisfactory information of the abandonment by the insurgents of such barbarous practices, shall revoke or modify said instructions. Congress do not, however, intend by this resolution to limit or restrict the power of the President to the modes or principles of retaliation herein mentioned, but only to advise a resort to them as demanded by the occasion.

Mr. Sumner offered the following Resolutions as a substitute for the Resolution of the Committee: —

Resolved, That retaliation is harsh always, even in the simplest cases, and is permissible only where, in the first place, it may reasonably be expected to effect its object, and where, in the second place, it is consistent with the usages of civilized society; and that, in the absence of these essential conditions, it is a useless barbarism, having no other end than vengeance, which is forbidden alike to nations and to men.

Resolved, That the treatment of our officers and soldiers in rebel prisons is cruel, savage, and heart-rending beyond all precedent; that it is shocking to morals; that it is an offence against human nature itself; that it adds

new guilt to the great crime of the rebellion, and constitutes an example from which history will turn with
sorrow and disgust.

Resolved, That any attempted imitation of rebel barbarism in the treatment of prisoners would be plainly
impracticable, on account of its inconsistency with the
prevailing sentiments of humanity among us ; that it
would be injurious at home, for it would barbarize the
whole community ; that it would be utterly useless, for it
could not affect the cruel authors of the revolting conduct
which we seek to overcome ; that it would be immoral,
inasmuch as it proceeded from vengeance alone ; that it
could have no other result than to degrade the national
character and the national name, and to bring down upon
our country the reprobation of history ; and that, being
thus impracticable, useless, immoral, and degrading, it
must be rejected as a measure of retaliation, precisely as
the barbarism of roasting or eating prisoners is always
rejected by civilized powers.

Resolved, That the United States, filled with grief
and sympathy for cherished citizens, who, as officers
and soldiers, have become the victims of Heaven-defying
outrage, hereby declare their solemn determination to put
an end to this great iniquity by putting an end to the
rebellion of which it is the natural fruit; that to secure
this humane and righteous consummation, they pledge
anew their best energies and all the resources of the
whole people, and they call upon all to bear witness that,
in this necessary warfare with barbarism, they renounce
all vengeance and every evil example, and plant themselves firmly on the sacred landmarks of Christian civili-

zation, under the protection of that God who is present with every prisoner, and enables heroic souls to suffer for their country.

XV.

The pathetic letter, which was composed by the suffering and dying men at Andersonville, and addressed to the President in August, 1864, and forwarded by the prisoners who were sent to Charleston, led to renewed efforts on the part of the United States government; but no notice was taken by the rebel authorities of the plea in behalf of humanity. The following letter is said to be the one sent to the President: —

The Memorial of the Union Prisoners confined at Andersonville, Georgia, to the President of the United States.

CONFEDERATE STATES PRISON,
CHARLESTON, S. C., Aug., 1864.

TO THE PRESIDENT OF THE UNITED STATES:

The condition of the enlisted men belonging to the Union armies, now prisoners to the Confederate rebel forces, is such that it becomes our duty, and the duty of every commissioned officer, to make known the facts in the case to the government of the United States, and to use every honorable effort to secure a general exchange of prisoners, thereby relieving thousands of our comrades from the horror now surrounding them.

For some time past there has been a concentration of prisoners from all parts of the rebel territory to the State of Georgia — the commissioned officers being confined at Macon, and the enlisted men at Andersonville.

Recent movements of the Union armies under General Sherman have compelled the removal of prisoners to other points, and it is now understood that they will be removed to Savannah, Georgia, and Columbus and Charleston, South Carolina. But no change of this kind holds out any prospect of relief to our poor men. Indeed, as the localities selected are far more unhealthy, there must be an increase rather than a diminution of suffering.

Colonel Hill, provost-marshal general Confederate States army, at Atlanta, stated to one of the undersigned that there were thirty-five thousand prisoners at Andersonville, and by all accounts from the United States soldiers who have been confined there, the number is not overstated by him. These thirty-five thousand are confined in a field of some thirty acres, enclosed by a board fence, heavily guarded. About one third have various kinds of indifferent shelter, but upwards of thirty thousand are wholly without shelter, or even shade of any kind, and are exposed to the storms and rains which are of almost daily occurrence, the cold dews of the night, and the more terrible effects of the sun striking with almost tropical fierceness upon their unprotected heads. This mass of men jostle and crowd each other up and down the limits of their enclosure in storms or sun, and others lie down upon the pitiless earth at night with no other covering than the clothing upon their backs, few of them having even a blanket.

Upon entering the prison every man is deliberately stripped of money and other property, and as no clothing or blankets are ever supplied to their prisoners by the rebel authorities, the condition of the apparel of the soldiers, just from an active campaign, can be easily imagined. Thousands are without pants or coats, and hundreds without even a pair of drawers to cover their nakedness.

To these men, as indeed to all prisoners, there are issued three quarters of a pound of bread or meal, and one eighth of a pound of meat, per day. This is the entire ration, and upon it the prisoner must live or die. The meal is often unsifted and sour, and the meat such as in the North is consigned to the soap-maker. Such are the rations upon which Union soldiers are fed by the rebel authorities, and by which they are barely holding on to life. But to starvation, and exposure to sun and storm, add the sickness which prevails to a most alarming and terrible extent. On an average, one hundred die daily. It is impossible that any Union soldiers should know all the facts pertaining to this terrible mortality, as they are not paraded by the rebel authorities. Such statement as the following, made by —— ——, speaks eloquent testimony. Said he, " Of twelve of us who were captured, six died, four are in the hospital, and I never expect to see them again. There are but two of us left."

In 1862, at Montgomery, Alabama, under far more favorable circumstances, the prisoners being protected by sheds, from one hundred and fifty to two hundred were sick from diarrhœa and chills out of seven hundred. The same percentage would give seven thousand sick at Andersonville.

It needs no comment, no efforts at word-painting, to make such a picture stand out boldly in most horrible colors.

8

Nor is this all. Among the ill-fated of the many who
have suffered amputation in consequence of injuries received before capture, sent from rebel hospitals before
their wounds were healed, there are eloquent witnesses
of the barbarities of which they are victims. If to these
facts is added this, that nothing more demoralizes soldiers
and develops the evil passions of man than starvation,
the terrible condition of Union prisoners at Andersonville
can be readily imagined. They are fast losing hope and
becoming utterly reckless of life.

Numbers, crazed by their sufferings, wander about in a
state of idiocy; others deliberately cross the " dead line,"
and are remorselessly shot down.

In behalf of these men we most earnestly appeal to
the President of the United States. Few of them have
been captured, except in the front of battle, in the deadly
encounter, and only when overpowered by numbers.
They constitute as gallant a portion of our armies as
carry our banners anywhere. If released, they would
soon return to again do vigorous battle for our cause.
We are told that the only obstacle in the way of exchange
is the status of enlisted negroes captured from our armies,
the United States claiming that the cartel covers all who
who serve under its flag, and the Confederate States
refusing to consider the colored soldiers, heretofore slaves,
as prisoners of war.

We beg leave to suggest some facts bearing upon the
question of exchange, which we would urge upon this
consideration. Is it not consistent with the national
honor, without waiving the claim that the negro soldiers
shall be treated as prisoners of war, to effect an exchange

of the white soldiers? The two classes are treated differently by the enemy. The whites are confined in such prisons as Libby and Andersonville, starved and treated with a barbarism unknown to civilized nations. The blacks, on the contrary, are seldom imprisoned. They are distributed among the citizens, or employed on government works. Under these circumstances they receive enough to eat, and are worked no harder than they have been accustomed to be. They are neither starved nor killed off by the pestilence in the dungeons of Richmond and Charleston. It is true they are again made slaves; but their slavery is freedom and happiness compared with the cruel existence imposed upon our gallant men. They are not bereft of hope, as are the white soldiers, dying by piecemeal. Their chances of escape are tenfold greater than those of the white soldiers, and their condition, in all its lights, is tolerable in comparison with that of the prisoners of war now languishing in the dens and pens of secession.

While, therefore, believing the claims of our government, in matters of exchange, to be just, we are profoundly impressed with the conviction that the circumstances of the two classes of soldiers are so widely different that the government can honorably consent to an exchange, waiving for a time the established principle justly claimed to be applicable in the case. Let thirty-five thousand suffering, starving, and enlisted men aid this appeal. By prompt and decided action in their behalf, thirty-five thousand heroes will be made happy. For the eighteen hundred commissioned officers now prisoners we urge nothing. Although desirous of returning

to our duty, we can bear imprisonment with more forti-
tude if the enlisted men, whose sufferings we know to be
intolerable, were restored to liberty and life.

XVI.

The threatening manœuvres of Sherman alone caused
the rebel authorities to diminish the number of inmates
of this stockade, and thereby lessen the dangers of recap-
ture, and remove the temptation to the United States
authorities to make an effort for their rescue.   It has
been stated that the rebels were anxious to exchange prisoners, man for man, and that the obstructions were caused
by the Federal authorities, and that Mr. Stanton, in particular, was responsible for the stoppage of exchange and
the consequent death of so many thousands of our fellow-
citizens detained in the rebel prisons.

General Hitchcock, the United States commissioner
of exchange, however, denies most emphatically that Mr.
Stanton was any way responsible for the refusal to make
exchanges, man for man, officer for officer, according to
grade, and he makes the following statement: " At no
instance within my knowledge did Mr. Stanton refuse to
acquiesce in any proposition looking to that result.   There
is not in my office, nor have I ever seen such a proposition from a rebel commissioner or the rebel authorities.
Nor have I any reason to believe that any such proposition was ever made by Judge Ould, or any of his supe-
riors, except in a letter from Judge Ould addressed to
Major Mulford, which fell into the hands of Major-
General Butler.   This is true, emphatically, as a protec-

tion against the accusations levelled at Mr. Stanton. * · * * * * Mr. Stanton has not only been willing, but anxious to make exchanges referred to, as I have abundant means of showing by indisputable documents, the aim and purpose of Judge Ould was to draw from us all of the rebel prisoners held in exchange for white troops of the United States held as prisoners in the South, persistently refusing to exchange colored troops to a very late date; when, to carry a special purpose, he receded so far as to agree to exchange free colored men, leaving the general principle where it was on his side against the just claims of a large body of colored prisoners held in the South."

XVII.

The following letter from General Butler to the rebel commissioner of exchange will throw some light upon the subject, and give an idea as to whom the blame of non-exchange and non-intercourse belongs: —

Letter of Major-General Butler, United States Commissioner of Exchange, to Colonel Ould, the Confederate Commissioner.

HEADQUARTERS DEPARTMENT OF VIRGINIA AND NORTH
CAROLINA, IN THE FIELD, August, 1864.

HON. ROBERT OULD, *Commissioner of Exchange.*

SIR: Your note to Major Mulford, assistant agent of exchange, under date of 10th August, has been referred to me.

You therein state that Major Mulford has several times

proposed " to exchange prisoners respectively held by the two belligerents — officer for officer, and man for man," and that " the offer has also been made by other officials having charge of matters connected with the exchange of prisoners," and that " this proposal has been heretofore declined by the Confederate authorities." That you now " consent to the above proposition, and agree to deliver to you (Major Mulford) the prisoners held in captivity by the Confederate authorities, provided you agree to deliver an equal number of officers and men. As equal numbers are delivered from time to time they will be declared exchanged. This proposal is made with the understanding that the officers and men on both sides who have been longest in captivity will be first delivered, where it is practicable."

From a slight ambiguity in your phraseology, but more perhaps from the antecedent action of your authorities, and because of your acceptance of it, I am in doubt whether you have stated the proposition with entire accuracy.

It is true, a proposition was made both by Major Mulford and myself, as agent of exchange, to exchange all prisoners of war taken by either belligerent party, man for man, officer for officer, of equal rank, or their equivalents. It was made by me as early as the first of the winter of 1863–4, and has not been accepted. In May last I forwarded to you a note, desiring to know whether the Confederate authorities intended to treat colored soldiers of the United States army as prisoners of war. To that inquiry no answer has yet been made. To avoid all possible misapprehension or mistake hereafter as to your

offer now, will you now say whether you mean by " prisoners held in captivity " colored men, duly enrolled, and
mustered into the service of the United States, who have
been captured by the Confederate forces; and if your
authorities are willing to exchange all soldiers so mustered
into the United States army, whether colored or otherwise, and the officers commanding them, man for man,
officer for officer?

At the interview which was held between yourself and
the agent of exchange on the part of the United States
at Fortress Monroe, in March last, you will do me the
favor to remember the principal discussion turned upon
this very point; you, on behalf of the Confederate government, claiming the right to hold all negroes who had
heretofore been slaves, and not emancipated by their masters, enrolled and mustered into the service of the United
States, when captured by your forces, not as prisoners of
war, but upon capture to be turned over to their supposed
masters or claimants, whoever they might be, to be held
by them as slaves.

By the advertisements in your newspapers, calling upon
masters to come forward and claim these men so captured, I suppose that your authorities still adhere to that
claim — that is to say, that whenever a colored soldier of
the United States is captured by you, upon whom any
claim can be made by any person residing within the
States now in insurrection, such soldier is not to be treated
as a prisoner of war, but is to be turned over to his supposed owner or claimant, and put at such labor or service
as that owner or claimant may choose, and the officers in
command of such soldiers, in the language of a supposed

act of the Confederate States, are to be turned over to the governors of States, upon requisitions, for the purpose of being punished by the làws of such States for acts done in war in the armies of the United States.

You must be aware that there is still a proclamation by Jefferson Davis, claiming to be chief executive of the Confederate States, declaring in substance that all officers of colored troops mustered into the service of the United States were not to be treated as prisoners of war, but were to be turned over for punishment to the governors of States.

I am reciting these public acts from memory, and will be pardoned for not giving the exact words, although I believe I do not vary the substance and effect.

These declarations on the part of those whom you represent yet remain unrepealed, unannulled, unrevoked, and must therefore be still supposed to be authoritative.

By your acceptance of our proposition, is the government of the United States to understand that these several claims, enactments, and proclaimed declarations are to be given up, set aside, revoked, and held for nought by the Confederate authorities, and that you are ready and willing to exchange, man for man, those colored soldiers of the United States, duly mustered and enrolled as such, who have heretofore been claimed as slaves by the Confederate States, as well as white soldiers?

If this be so, and you are so willing to exchange these colored men claimed as slaves, and you will so officially inform the government of the United States, then, as I am instructed, a principal difficulty in effecting exchanges will be removed.

As I informed you personally, in my judgment it is neither consistent with the policy, dignity, or honor of the United States, upon any consideration, to allow those who, by our laws solemnly enacted, are made soldiers of the Union, and who have been duly enlisted, enrolled, and mustered as such soldiers, who have borne arms in behalf of this country, and who have been captured while fighting in vindication of the rights of that country, not to be treated as prisoners of war, and remain unchanged and in the service of those who claim them as masters; and I cannot believe that the government of the United States will ever be found to consent to so gross a wrong.

Pardon me if I misunderstand you in supposing that your acceptance of our proposition does not in good faith mean to include all the soldiers of the Union, and that you still intend, if your acceptance is agreed to, to hold the colored soldiers of the Union unexchanged, and at labor or service, because I am informed that very lately, almost contemporaneously with this offer on your part to exchange prisoners, and which seems to include *all* prisoners of war, the Confederate authorities have made a declaration that the negroes heretofore held to service by owners in the States of Delaware, Maryland, and Missouri are to be treated as prisoners of war, when captured in arms in the service of the United States.

Such declaration that a part of the colored soldiers of the United States were to be prisoners of war, would seem most strongly to imply that others were not to be so treated, or, in other words, that the colored men from the insurrectionary States are to be held to labor and returned to their masters, if captured by the Confederate

8 *

forces while duly enrolled and mustered into and actually in the armies of the United States.

In the view which the government of the United States
takes of the claim made by you to the persons and services of these negroes, it is not to be supported upon any
principle of national and municipal law.

Looking upon these men only as property upon your
theory of property in them, we do not see how this claim
can be made, certainly not how it can be yielded. It is
believed to be a well-settled rule of public international law,
and a custom and part of the laws of war, that the capture
of movable property vests the title to that property in the
captor, and therefore where one belligerent gets into full
possession property belonging to the subjects or citizens
of the other belligerent, the owner of that property is at
once divested of his title, which rests in the belligerent
government capturing and holding such possessions.
Upon this rule of international law all civilized nations
have acted, and by it both belligerents have dealt with all
property, save slaves, taken from each other during the
present war.

If the Confederate forces capture a number of horses
from the United States, the animals are claimed to be,
and, as we understand it, become the property of the
Confederate authorities.

If the United States capture any movable property in
the rebellion, by our regulations and laws, in conformity
with international law and the laws of war, such property is turned over to our government as its property.
Therefore, if we obtain possession of that species of property known to the laws of the insurrectionary States as

slaves, why should there be any doubt that that property, like any other, vests in the United States?

If the property in the slave does so vest, then the *jus disponendi*, the right of disposing of that property, vests in the United States.

Now, the United States have disposed of the property which they have acquired by capture in slaves taken by them, i. e., by emancipating them, and declaring them free forever; so that, if we have not mistaken the principles of international law and the laws of war, we have no slaves in the armies of the United States. All are free men, being made so in such manner as we have chosen to dispose of our property in them which we acquired by capture.

Slaves being captured by us, and the right of property in them thereby vested in us, that right of property has been disposed of by us by manumitting them, as has already been the acknowledged right of the owner to do to his slave. The manner in which we dispose of our property while it is in our possession certainly cannot be questioned by you. Nor is the case altered if the property is not actually captured in battle, but comes either voluntarily or involuntarily from the belligerent owner into the possession of the other belligerent.

I take it no one would doubt the right of the United States to a drove of Confederate mules or a herd of Confederate cattle which should wander or rush across the Confederate lines into the lines of the United States army. So it seems to me, treating the negro as property merely, if that piece of property passes the Confederate lines, and comes into the lines of the United States, that property is as much lost to its owner in the Confederate States as would be the mule or ox, the property of the resident of the Confederate States, which should fall into our hands.

If, therefore, the privilege of international law and the laws of war used in this discussion are correctly stated, then it would seem that the deduction logically flows therefrom in natural sequence, that the Confederate States can have no claim upon the negro soldiers captured by them from the armies of the United States because of the former ownership of them by their citizens or subjects, and only claim such as result, under the laws of war, from their captor merely.

Do the Confederate authorities claim the right to reduce to a state of slavery free men, prisoners of war captured by them? This claim our fathers fought against under Bainbridge and Decatur, when set up by the Barbary Powers on the northern shore of Africa, about the year 1800, — and in 1864 their children will hardly yield it upon their own soil.

This point I will not pursue further, because I understand you to repudiate the idea that you will reduce free men to slaves because of capture in war, and that you base the claim of the Confederate authorities to re-enslave our negro soldiers, when captured by you, upon the *jus postliminii*, or that principle of the law of nations which inhabilitates the former owner with his property taken by an enemy when such property is recovered by the forces of his own country. Or, in other words, you claim that, by the laws of nations and of war, when property of the subjects of one belligerent power, captured by the forces of the other belligerent, is recaptured by the armies of the former owner, then such property is to be restored to its prior possessor, as if it had never been captured ; and, therefore, under this principle, your authorities propose to restore to their masters the slaves which heretofore belonged to them which you may capture from us.

But this postliminary right under which you claim to act, as understood and defined by all writers on national law, is applicable simply to *immovable property*, and that, too, only after complete resubjugation of that portion of the country in which the property is situated, upon which this right fastens itself. By the laws and customs of war, this right has never been applied to *movable* property. True it is, I believe, that the Romans attempted to apply it to the case of slaves; but for two thousand years no other nation has attempted to set up this right as ground for treating slaves differently from other property.

But the Romans even refused to re-enslave men captured from opposing belligerents in a civil war, such as ours unhappily is.

Consistently, then, with any principle of the law of nations, treating slaves as property merely, it would seem to be impossible for the government of the United States to permit the negroes in their ranks to be re-enslaved when captured, or treated otherwise than as prisoners of war.

I have forborne, sir, in this discussion, to argue the question upon any other or different ground of right than those adopted by your authorities in claiming the negro as property, because I understand that your fabric of opposition to the government of the United States has the right of property in man as its corner-stone. Of course, it would not be profitable in settling a question of exchange of prisoners of war to attempt to argue the question of abandonment of the very corner-stone of their attempted political edifice. Therefore I have admitted all the considerations which should apply to the negro soldier as a man, and dealt with him upon the Confederate theory of property only.

I unite with you most cordially, sir, in desiring a speedy settlement of all these questions, in view of the great suffering endured by our prisoners in the hands of your authorities, of which you so feelingly speak. Let me ask, in view of that suffering, why you have delayed eight months to answer a proposition which by now accepting you admit to be right, just, and humane, allowing that suffering to continue so long? One cannot help thinking, even at the risk of being deemed uncharitable, that the benevolent sympathies of the Confederate authorities have been lately stirred by the depleted condition of their armies, and a desire to get into the field, to affect the present campaign, the hale, hearty, and well-fed prisoners held by the United States in exchange for the half-starved, sick, emaciated, and unserviceable soldiers of the United States now languishing in your prisons. The events of this war, if we did not know it before, have taught us that it is not the northern people alone who know how to drive sharp bargains.

The wrongs, indignities, and privations suffered by our soldiers would move me to consent to anything to procure their exchange, except to barter away the honor and faith of the government of the United States, which has been so solemnly pledged to the colored soldiers in its ranks.

Consistently with national faith and justice we cannot relinquish this position. With your authorities it is a question of property merely. It seems to address itself to you in this form: Will you suffer your soldier, captured in fighting your battles, to be in confinement for months rather than release him by giving for him that which you call a piece of property, and which we are willing to accept as a man?

You certainly appear to place less value upon your soldier than you do upon your negro. I assure you, much as we of the North are accused of loving property, our citizens would have no difficulty in yielding up any piece of property they have in exchange for one of their brothers or sons languishing in your prisons. Certainly there could be no doubt that they would do so, were that piece of property less in value than five thousand dollars in Confederate money, which is believed to be the price of an able-bodied negro in the insurrectionary States.

Trusting that I may receive such a reply to the questions propounded in this note as will tend to a speedy resumption of the negotiations in a full exchange of all prisoners, and a delivery of them to their respective authorities,

I have the honor to be,

Very respectfully,

Your obedient servant,

BENJAMIN F. BUTLER,

Major-General and Commissioner of Exchange.

XVIII.

The wretched " material" exchanged for healthy rebel
soldiers called forth a note of joy from the rebel commissioner, Ould.   The exchanged Federal soldiers were half-
naked, " living skeletons," covered with filth and vermin ;
and nearly all of them were unfit for service or labor, and
most of them physically ruined for the remainder of their
lives.   The flag-of-truce boats of the different parties presented terrible contrasts.   On the one were to be seen
feeble, emaciated, ragged, filthy, and dying men from the
rebel prisons ; whilst on the other were the rebels returning from our prisons, well clad in our uniforms, strong
and healthy from the abundance of food.   We returned
men who had been well treated, and who were then ready
to take the field again ; whilst we received in turn abused
and decrepit soldiers, who were so much reduced and
weakened that few, comparatively, ever again returned to
service.   Along the entire line of prison stockades, from
Belle Isle in Virginia to Prison Tyler in Texas, the same
story is told of fiendish cruelty.

More than thirty thousand of our soldiers have un-
doubtedly perished during, or in consequence of the barbarities of their prison life in the South.   To ascertain
the precise number will be a difficult task, for many of
the returned prisoners have died since they have left the
service ; but when we consider the number of prisons,
and the long period of occupation, we think that the estimate of thirty thousand is not too high.

XIX.

When General Stoneman made his attempt to rescue the prisoners, Winder issued the order No. 13, which stamps the brute with infamy beyond redemption. In this order, which has been preserved, Winder commanded the officers in charge of the artillery to open their batteries, loaded with grape-shot, as soon as the Federals approached within seven miles, and to continue the slaughter until every prisoner was exterminated. Similar threats were made all along the line of the prison stockades in North Carolina and in Virginia. "Was the prison mined," said Colonel Farnsworth to Turner, the jailer of Libby Prison, "when General Kilpatrick approached Richmond to attempt to rescue the prisoners?" "Yes," was the brutal reply; "and I would have blown you all to Hades before I would have suffered you to be rescued." Twelve hundred men blown into atoms at one explosion! Thirty thousand men to be torn into shreds by the iron bullets of the cannon! Contrast the orders of these chivalric men with that of Aboukere, the chief of a reputed barbarous horde of Bedouins of the desert: —

"Warriors of Islam! attend a moment, and listen well to the precepts which I am about to promulge to you for observation in times of war. Fight with bravery and loyalty. Never use artifice or perfidy towards your enemies. Do not mutilate the fallen. Do not slay the aged, nor the children, nor the women. You will find upon your route men living in solitude, in meditation, in the adoration of God: do them no injury, give them no offence."

In which are the evidences the most positive of a fraternal religion and an advanced civilization?

XX.

Even women and young girls came from distances to view the spectacle. They climbed the parapets of the earthworks, and gloated and made merry over the scene of suffering. They threw crusts of bread over the palisades to see the starving wretches struggle for the morsel of life.

They even reviled the condition of the dying. This surpasses the ferocity, the depravity, the wickedness of gladiatorial times. " The fury of women when once excited," says the French historian, " soon rises to profanation and excess." When the love of humanity vanishes from our breasts, it is the death of nature.

There were, however, a few noble exceptions to those strange acts of delight in cruelty; and the deeds of kindness of a few women in other parts of the South shine with increased brilliancy from the terrible contrast.

XXI.

Several of the papers of the South openly and unhesitatingly approved of the methods of their prison depletion, and gloated over the fearful destitution and mortality.

The Macon " Telegraph and Confederate," only the day before the surrender of the city to the Federal forces, justified the atrocities at Andersonville; and the Rich-

mond " Examiner " exclaimed, " Let the Yankee prisoners be put where the cold weather and scant fare will
thin them out in accordance with the laws of nature."
There were, however, noble exceptions to the general
exhibition of ferocity; and several officers of the rebel
army did declare that the condition of affairs at Andersonville was a " reproach to them as a nation."

The author, who served for five years in the Federal
armies of Virginia, of the South, and the South-west, and
whose opportunities for observation and inquiry were extensive, does not believe General Lee to be implicated in
these outrages. It is true that Lee might have openly and
boldly protested against the barbarities, and gained thereby the admiration and the blessing of mankind; but he
knew full well that the remonstrance would have fallen
upon the cold ear of the implacable executive with no
more effect and weight than when the snow-flake falls
upon the Alps.

The Virginian struggled to hold his own against the
selfish and jealous ambition of the remorseless Mississip-
pian.

To have participated in the revolting cabal of cruelty,
there was required the baseness of political intrigue, and
to this depth the soldier never sank.

XXII.

To charge an entire people with barbarity, because its
rulers sanction crime, and a vile and venal press applaud
the motives and the deeds, should not be maintained
without long deliberation. " History has the right of

suspecting without evidence, but never of accusing without proof." The rank and file of the rebel army were
drawn from the classes of poor whites, who were essentially rural in their populations, and who possessed some
trace of the morals and the natural sentiments of generosity that belong to people who cultivate the earth. Although their instincts were modified by the contact of
slave labor, they never sank so low in the social scale —
to that level of the vile populace of the Roman or medieval times, when the crimes of the emperors were applaud-
ed. These men on the battle-field exhibited feelings of
humanity; and it was only under the direction of their
leaders that they became unkind and ferocious.

It was the leaders who were responsible for the crimes
of the sedition ; and what of humanity could be expected
from men degenerated in blood? What of noble intelligence could be looked for from mental faculties long since
degraded?· What evidence of a Christian spirit could be
hoped for from men who had openly perverted or denied
all the divine precepts, upon which revolve the well-being
of the human race? " If we had triumphed," says one of
its apostles, at this late day of forgiveness and repent-
ance — " if we had triumphed, I should have favored strip-
ping them naked. Pardon! They might have appealed
for pardon, but I would have seen them damned before I
would have granted it ! "

When Suwarrow forced his way by the sword into the
heart of Poland, dividing the realm, devastating the land,
and destroying multitudes of people, he offered blasphe-
mous thanks to Heaven for victories obtained over men
fighting in the sacred cause of liberty, and for all the
human heart holds dear.

XXIII.

To judge correctly of the magnitudes of these immolations, these crimes, history must wait for a calmer period,
when prejudice shall have relaxed its hold upon the understanding, and when time shall have rolled up its accumulated materials of accusation and denial, of proof and
exoneration. At present we can form some idea of their
designs, and the degree of the implacability of their souls,
from the evidence already placed before us, as we measure
inaccessible heights by the awful shadows which they
project.

Pity appears to have been with them only a vain, fleet-
ing emotion, if the soul was disturbed at all ; and whenever an act of humanity was displayed, there seems to
have been the secret motive of gain at work. In defining
the natural sentiments of pity, they would have declared
them the illusions of the imagination.

The brutalizing scenes of Slavery had modified and
affected their natural feelings, as the gladiatorial combats
and exposures of the Christians to the attacks of infuriated wild beasts had inspired the vile populace of Rome
with the love of blood and cruelty.

When these men, with sonorous rhetoric, proclaimed
themselves as the guiding minds of the republic, the
patrons, the judges of the correct ideas and principles of
civilization, — when they arrogated to themselves the appearance of the wisdom of Lacedæmon with the politeness of Athens, — they forgot or despised those cardinal
virtues of society, " justice and truth — these are the first
duties of man ; humanity, country — these his first affections."

XXIV.

" I fear," writes the rebel War Clerk, observing from his secure position in the war office, " I fear this government in future times will be denounced as a cabal of bandits and outlaws, making and executing the most despotic decrees."

Whether this system of the reduction of prisoners was devised by the executive, or his immediate advisers, time may reveal. But of this we may remain positive, that the crime belongs to that little faction of Breckinridge Democrats who ruled the Confederacy as they pleased, and of which Davis was the recognized leader. Wirz was only the De Vargas and Winder the Alva of the arranged system. Neither is there any doubt that the power of affording relief was clearly within the control of the executive. This power was not withheld from want of audacity, for the man who dared place in power, in spite of remonstrance, men who jeopardized the existence of the Confederacy, and who openly disgraced its honor, certainly had sufficient courage to perform a common act of humanity, and relieve the sufferings of tortured prisoners, if such had been his inclination.

No; there was a system, and " systems are brutal forces." " What are your laws and theories," said Danton, brutally, to Gensonné, " when the only law is to triumph, and the sole theory for the nation is the theory of existence." — " Give a man power of doing what he pleases with impunity, you extinguish his fear, and consequently overturn in him one of the great pillars of morality. This, too, we find confirmed by matter of fact.

How many hopeful heirs-apparent to grand empires, when in possession of them, have become such monsters of lust and cruelty as are a reproach to human nature!" — "Ambition brings to men dissimulation, perfidy, the art of feigning the language and sentiments which lay at the bottom of the heart; of measuring their hate and their friendship only by their interests and circumstances; and above all, the perfidious science of composing their features, rather than correct and govern their principles."

The wills of bad men are their laws, and brute strength their logic.

XXV.

It is only distance in time that separates and distinguishes the Caligulas of history, the early, medieval, and present periods. History exhibits the first as the undisguised monster of atrocity. The last, overshadowed by the mantle of the law, stands but partially revealed.

To the perverted imaginations of the first the senate presented no force of resistance. To the petulant asperity, the abuse of power of the last, the doubtful liberties of the people imposed certain restrictions, which led to the resort of narrow and malignant minds — secrecy and concealment.

Nature had not cast him in the mould of those statesmen who sacrifice all personal feelings for the public good, and who willingly yield up their lives to advance the noble work of true civilization. Obstinacy with him was firmness; cunning, depth; resistance to humane feelings, resolution. Envy, hatred, murmurs, were braved with inflexible determination when pursuing his plans of favoritism, or defending his tools of oppression and cruelty against the voice of nature and outraged liberty.

There are some men who appear to be destined for the instruction of the world, as the abettors and satellites of despotism, who cannot or who do not recognize the difference between interest or conscience ; who desire to debase mankind, that they may appear above the common level of humanity, conscious of their incapability of lifting themselves up by virtue and by nobility of action.

This man was the incarnation of the spirit of Slavery; he could have exclaimed, with Barnave, " Perish the colonies rather than a principle." This man was, for the time being, the entire incorporation of the sedition — its principles, its passions, its impulses, its cruelties.

"There are abysses which we dare not sound, and characters we desire not to fathom, for fear of finding in them too great darkness, too much horror."

This man, so calm, so dignified, so wise in his exterior, could not find sufficient generosity in his soul, although the representative of five millions of men, to say to these armies of suffering prisoners, * * * *indignus Cæsaris iræ* — unworthy of the anger of Cæsar.

XXVI.

What have the wretches to offer in atonement for these outrages upon nature, these violations of the spirit and majesty of the law, from which they now claim protection?

Will the blood of these living monsters expiate the martyrdom of the host of dead heroes? No!

Will it give ease or bring congratulation to the broken and aching hearts who yet revere the memory of the thirty thousand victims? Never!

The divine spirit of liberty would protest against the defilement of her sacred altars with the foul blood of such filthy and depraved sacrifices.

Let the gates of the prison open, and these men stand forth to the full gaze of offended mankind, assassins and murderers as they are.

Vengeance does not belong to the human race.

There are times in the history of men when human invectives are without force. "There are deeds of which no men are judges, and which mount, without appeal, direct to the tribunal of God."

9

BOOK EIGHTH.

I.

CERTAIN branches of the human family present physical peculiarities and aptitudes for certain climates which others do not. The one thrives and arrives at perfection, whilst the other languishes and dies.

Floras and Faunas have well-defined limits of latitude, beyond which they decline and become extinct, and in some countries we observe certain limitations as to longitudes. "There are tropical trees that become shrubs in our zone, and the flowers of our meadows have their types in the tapering trunks of other climes."

How rapidly the beautiful varieties of domestic animals deteriorate and disappear when removed from the localities and conditions in which they attained their excellence. The handsome Swiss cattle when carried to the plains of Lombardy, and the remarkable varieties of the English herds when removed to Central France, quickly lose their characteristics of form and superiority. Under the tropics the sheep loses its silken fleece, and the noble qualities of the dog greatly change.

Even the insect world changes greatly in every twelve degrees of latitude, and an alteration, almost total, appears in double the space.

The influence of climate and locality, which exercises so positive a power in the vegetable kingdom and animal reign, affects man likewise, and would be as distinctly marked were it not resisted by the forces of the intelligence. We find under certain parallels of latitude more energy of mind and greater activity of body than at others ; we observe this more distinctly with particular races or varieties than with others, thus indicating that all have not the same aptitudes : again, through a combination of organic and social laws, types adapted to certain pursuits spring up in every civilized country, these types distinct from either varieties or species. We also see the sharp characteristics of races, when migrating, become less distinct, and mixtures increase, and the inferior races disappear, like "the elementary language or the primitive forms of the social state."

The observed limit of range of the Hindoo and the African, in the Old World, is not beyond 30° of the equator, and in a lower latitude than 36° the European colonies have never prospered, never succeeded, in their attempts for empire. Where now are the countless hosts of Romans, Gauls, and Vandals that have occupied Northern Africa in past times? The ethnologist of to-day cannot discover a feature, hardly a trace even, of the language of the conquerors remaining among the present tribes of occupation. Even the Roman has vanished, and the only vestige of the Carthaginian and Numidian is shown by the scattered and diminished Bergers. These varieties contended with the climate, and were gradually absorbed by the stronger native tribes.

The Mongols once held Central Europe, the Goths

ruled Italy. Where are they? There is no longer Vandalic blood in Africa or Gothic blood in Italy.

In later times the strong, the fierce and dauntless Northmen held the Sicilies, and as the incorruptible Varingar guarded and upheld with their fearless swords the waning empire of the effeminate Greeks at the Dardanelles. Where are they and their descendants? The only traces are seen among the tombstones at Palermo, or in the Runic inscriptions which they sacrilegiously sculptured with their long blades of steel upon the flanks of the marble lion of the Piræus.

II.

In the year 1600 hardly a European family could be found along the headlands and indentations of the coast which form the southern limit of the Slave States of America.

Since that time the countless multitudes of the red men who inhabited the forests of these lands have disappeared, and other races from an older world and other climes have taken their places, increasing in numbers with as great rapidity as the other declined.

We have seen here the swarthy sons of Nubia, under the fostering care of Slavery, or under the mysterious and unexplained influences of climate, increase with such rapidity, that the ratio for the last decade (previous to the war), if continued for a century, would give a black population of more than forty millions. Strange spectacle in the movement of races!

Here we see, almost during the memory of living men,

a distinct race disappear, and a new nation of totally opposite character rise up, as if by magic, in their vanishing footsteps. How prophetic was the speech of the Indian chief to his tribe, when he beheld with dismay the steady progress of the white men who lived upon the cereals! "I say, then," exclaimed the red man, "to every one who hears me, before the trees above our heads shall have died of age, before the maples of the valley cease to yield us sugar, the race of the sowers of corn will have extirpated the race of flesh-eaters."

III.

This rate of increase observed among the blacks of our Slave States is not seen among the population of the West India Islands, where singular oscillations are exhibited, and the statistics of the past two centuries have inclined two of the most eminent European statisticians to assert that in a century the negro will nearly have disappeared from these islands.

Observations at Martinique and Guadaloupe certainly warrant the inference. In Cuba the blacks decreased four or five thousand during the period of 1804 to 1817.

This decrease or stand-still in the progress of the race in these regions may have been caused by conditions, moral or physical, wholly within the control of man.

There are animals who will not propagate and continue their species whilst in a state of servitude, and it is reasonable to believe that the same moral causes affect the condition of enslaved mankind. Naturalists have shown how the evils of Slavery degrade animals, and

Buffon has pointed out the deep and conspicuous impressions it has made upon the camel.

IV.

Since the discovery and forcible entrance of the golden Empire of Mexico, and the display of her marvellous mineral treasures by the bold Cortez and his companions, we have seen a constant stream of the Spaniards and the affiliated nations of the Latin race pouring across the Atlantic to the new worlds which were given to the house of Castile and Leon by the sublime genius of the Genoese, following the stars and the traditions of the Northmen.

Wealth and the baseless fabrics of martial glory were the alluring objects of this migrating column of men.

" Hast thou gold?" exclaimed they to the Mexican princes. "I and my companions have a malady which is only cured by gold."

After these four centuries of occupation of the elevated plains and table-lands of Mexico, where the mean temperature does not exceed 77° Fahrenheit, and where the mildness of climate, the wealth of a wonderful, prolific nature, excite the ambition and the cupidity of men; and after the long efforts at colonization, in which the parent country was almost exhausted by the drain of her best blood, — Spain finds that the predictions of Dr. Knox are rapidly being realized, and that only 600,000 Europeans and their hybrid descendants, and but 8000 Spaniards of pure blood, can be found of all the numberless hosts that have embarked for these lands. Spain halts, and reflects upon this report of her scientific commission, which shows a decrease of one half since the estimate of Humboldt, in 1793; whilst France, always blind to reason whenever the eagles of glory desire to expand their wings, persists in her useless occupation of Algeria, where Gaul has again and again vainly endeavored to rear her colonies in times past; and she now attempts to unfurl her standards and establish her institutions on those Mexican shores where the blood and energy of a stronger and better adapted people have been expended in vain. Idle effort! The elements of nature are stronger than the will of men; neither do they give way to the desires or attacks of human ambition.

There are geographical boundaries which races cannot pass in pursuit of wealth or the dreams of ambition. A single generation will not determine the law of expansion and decay.

v.

In this connection it will be proper to glance over the past, among those phenomena which men have observed, and those laws which the Creator has thus far revealed to us for guidance in the procession of races or the march of intellect.

In the mysteries of the material world everything is governed by fixed and positive laws. Not a flower appears in the field to gladden the hearts of men but what rises up with invariable structure, and blooms at definite periods. Not a sparrow falls to the earth but in accordance with Nature's law. Not a star shines in the firmament but in unison with the great and illimitable designs of God. Everywhere do we observe harmony in space, in movement; everywhere visible signs of a beneficent, protecting Creator. It is the same with the enormous forms of living animals as with the insignificant shapes of the insect world: all play their part in the problem of Nature. Size is nothing with the Creator; form is nothing. Perchance

> " the poor beetle, that we tread upon,
> In corporal sufferance feels a pang as great
> As when a giant dies."

VI.

History indicates mysterious laws in the progress of the typical stocks of the human families; and it shows, in the colonization of the past, how frail are human calculations in migration and settlement unless based upon science. "It is not unknown to me," said the Roman soldier, two thousand years ago, when about to attack the remnant of the army of Brennus, that had passed over into Asia Minor, and conquered the land by the fierceness of their attack, and the terror of their name, — "it is not unknown to me," said Manlius, "that of all the nations inhabiting Asia, the Gauls have the highest reputation as soldiers.

"A fierce nation, after overrunning the face of the earth with its arms, has fixed its abode in the midst of a race of men the gentlest in the world. Their tall persons; their long, red hair; their vast shields, and swords of enormous length; their songs also when they are advancing to action; their yells and dances, and the horrid clashing of their arrows while they brandish their shields in a peculiar manner practised in their original country, — all these are circumstances calculated to strike terror. But let Greeks, and Phrygians, and Carians, who are unaccustomed to and unacquainted with these things, be frightened by such. The Romans, long acquainted with Gallic tumults, have learned the emptiness of their parade. Our forefathers had to deal with genuine native Gauls; but they are now a degenerate, a mongrel race, and in reality what they are named, Gallogrecians. Just so is the case of vegetables, the seeds not being so efficacious for preserving their original constitution as the properties of the soil and climate in which they may be reared, when changed, are towards altering it. The Macedonians who settled at Alexandria, in Egypt, or in Seleucia, or Babylonia, or in any other of their colonies scattered over the world, have sunk into Syrians, Parthians, or Egyptians.

"What trace do the Tarentines retain of the hardy, rugged discipline of Sparta? Everything that grows in its own natural soil attains the greater perfection: whatever is planted in a foreign land, by a gradual change in its nature degenerates into a similitude to that which affords it nurture. Brutes retain for a time, when taken, their natural ferocity; but after being long fed by the hands of men, they grow tame. Think ye then that Nature does not act in the same manner in softening the savage tempers of men? Do you believe these to be of the same kind that their fathers and grandfathers were?

* * * " By the very great fertility of the soil, the very

9 *

great mildness of the climate, and the gentle dispositions of the neighboring nations, all that barbarous fierceness which they brought with them has been quite mollified."

And finally the Romans themselves, in spite of their sanitary measures, became from year to year more alien in blood from the genuine stock of Romulus and Remus, until the distinctive characters of the conquerors of the earth finally disappeared.

The Latins, Sabines, and primitive Etruscans pressed constantly upon them with the irresistible force of destiny. When Scipio Æmilianus was interrupted in the forum by this mongrel populace, he exclaimed, " Silence, false sons of Italy ! Think ye to scare me with your brandished hands, ye whom I led myself in bonds to Rome?"

When the fierce and hardy Northmen descended into Southern Europe, they carried along with their laws a chastity and a reserve that excited universal surprise. But these virtues were not of long continuance there ; the climate and the customs of the new society soon warmed their frozen imaginations, and their laws by degrees relaxed, and their manners even more than their laws.

The giants of the North many times swept down over the plains of Italy, and regenerated with fresh and pure blood the puny breeds of degenerate Rome, but they have since disappeared, and their descendants are no longer to be found in these countries.

VII.

In relation to the futile efforts of Spain in Mexico, the ethnologist Knox exclaims, " Neither climate, nor government, nor external influences ever alter race. They may and they do affect them, and in time destroy them, but they never give rise to a new race. In half a century the dreams of Humboldt, of Canning, of Guizot, and other profound statesmen, have come to a close, and Nature once more, as I long ago predicted, asserts her rights."

Naturalists, from Hippocrates to Buffon, have believed that climate, heat and cold, dryness and humidity, the qualities and abundance of nourishment, have power to modify men and animals, but " neither climate, nor government, nor external circumstances ever give rise to a new race." The generous qualities once gone, are departed forever, and their loss can rarely be retrieved. Where is the instance of a fallen man, class, or nation?

" The history of nations," writes the Registrar-General of England, — " the history of nations on the Mediterranean or the plains of the Euphrates and Tigris, the deltas of the Indies and Ganges, and the rivers of China, exhibits the great fact: the gradual descent of race from the highlands, their establishment on the coasts, in cities sustained and refreshed for a season by emigration from the interior — their degradation in successive generations under the influence of the unhealthy earth, and their final ruin, effacement, or subjugation by new races of conquerors. The causes that destroy individual men lay cities waste, which, in their nature, are immortal, and silently undermine eternal empires.

> " A thousand years scarce serve to form a state ;
> An hour may lay it in the dust : and when
> Can man its shattered splendors renovate,
> Recall its virtues back, and vanquish time and fate ? "

VIII.

During this period of two centuries of colonization the European races have attempted to perpetuate their families upon these lands in question. They brought with them strong physical forces, and a high degree of mental cultivation. Mental strength will endure extremes of climate to a singular degree, but even this gradually yields to cosmic influences. It is a well-observed law of Nature that man must be organized in harmony with the condition of climate, otherwise he perishes. This scale of the strength of resisting opposing forces depends greatly upon the purity of the blood and the cultivation of the mind, whose remarkable powers of resisting disease have been observed and pointed out by Malte-Brun, Goethe, Kant, and other philosophers.

Europeans may visit and remain for limited periods in almost every portion of the globe. The deadly miasms of Central America, the pestilential atmospheres of Central Africa, and the frozen mists of either pole, are braved by the inquiring travellers of the civilized races, but not with impunity.

Intelligent and educated men may live for a while as gentlemen of leisure, in the midst of malarial climates, almost without perceptible effect, but the moment they apply their forces to the cultivation of the earth, Nature asserts her rights.

Yet during the period of the rich man, whilst he lives without physical labor, in ease, contemplation, and contentment, degeneration is slowly but surely taking place. The law of fecundity proves it, as with the Mamelukes in Egypt, as observed by Volney.

The English race loses its energy, according to Farr, in two or three generations in the lowlands of the West India Islands and in Southern Asia. The Duke of Wellington believed that every English family in Lower Bengal would die out in the third generation.

IX.

The laws of nature as regards influences of climate, food, and society, have operated less upon the condition of the rich slaveholder than the poorer white, who has struggled for existence, contending with the poverty of sterile or abandoned soils, and the hostile influences of climate, and the sneer of the slave and his master. The rich man has resisted the opposing forces of the elements with less apparent changes, whilst the poor man has succumbed to the influences and sadly degenerated, but the poor white still possesses the rough nobility and majesty of natural man, whilst the rich slaveholder, with his perverted ideas of honor, virtue, and justice, has gained the merited contempt of mankind. For the one, civilization has the sympathetic feeling of compassion; from the other, Nature herself recoils in horror.

This degeneration of the poor white is no mystery. Their poverty of blood and weakness of mind were not engendered by the insalubrity of climate, nor even by the sterility of the soil alone. Deny to any race, class, or community free social condition, freedom of thought, the expansion of the mind, the liberty of political and religious ideas, and it is sure to degenerate, and in time to perish.

The doctrine of Adam Smith and the theory of Malthus as to the fatal necessity of starvation, are in some measure correct, but they are mistaken in the view that human fecundity tends to get the start of the means of subsistence, for on the contrary it keeps pace with it.

We find that the fishes in the lakes, and the wolves in the forests, increase in exact ratio to the amount of food furnished. Nature regulates the fecundity of animals and human beings when society neglects it.

x.

The influences of climate, of food, of temperature, of domesticity upon the variation of species is well known. These mediate and external causes act with more vigor when the immediate and internal causes favor the effect. "All the mechanism of the formation of varieties," says Flourens, "turns upon these two internal causes — the tendency of the species to vary, and the transmission of the acquired variations." Cultivated plants and domesticated animals, when deprived of the modifying influence of man, return to the state of nature, and undergo new modifications, alterations, degenerations, even so far as to disguise and conceal the primitive type.

A few generations suffice to restore a variety to the primitive stock without retaining any of the organic elements which would debase it.

The more the influence of civilized man makes itself felt, the more the superior species overpower, absorb, or modify the inferior species.

The more rude the people and the less polished their

societies, the more powerful and rapid will be the influences of climate. Civilized men are continually exercising their talents to conform their conditions to the necessities of the time and place, and by their ingenuity remedy the defects, and by the resisting powers of a cultivated and occupied mind resist many of the morbid influences of climate. But plants and animals succumb at once if not protected by man.

XI.

During the more than two centuries of occupation of these southern lands there appear sufficient data to form, perhaps, some definite ideas of the success or failure of colonization, and the vague and doubtful process of acclimation. These evidences, thus far, are decidedly in favor of the black man. For he has multiplied with astonishing rapidity, and preserved his physical forces, and during this long and brutalizing term of his servitude he has not exhibited the ferocity of his master, save when hunted down like the beasts of prey, as in Hayti; neither has he sunk so low in the scale of true humanity as those who have held him in bondage.

The hungry and maimed soldier of the republic, escaping from the murderous prison-dens of the rebels, always found a crust of bread, a protecting shelter, and a kind word from the humblest and most oppressed of these beings.

Never were they betrayed by the black man, although the reward was large. Never were they denied assistance, although the penalty was death.

Although history seems to forbid, we are not of that class of men who maintain that there are inferior races, intended by nature for servitude ; for we believe that every race contains the elements of greatness, and that there is a common destiny to all. And we cherish the idea that there is a better future even for the black man among the civilized nations of the earth. The singular aptitude of the black man for music, which is the language of the soul ; his deep, sincere, immovable veneration for the precepts, the faith, the hope of Christianity, do not indicate a race lost to the nobler impulses, or to the benign influences of civilization, nor a people abandoned and accursed by Providence. God has gifted every living creature with the instinct of self-preservation ; he has endowed all animated creatures of the human form with the love of the beautiful, with the desire of developing and perfecting their innate powers, and of leaving on earth some act, some memorial worthy of imitation or remembrance. He who declines to help his fellow-creature in the struggle for social existence, in the effort for happiness, knowledge, and immortality, is less than a man.

The problem of civilization is left mostly to the free will of men, and God blasts and crumbles into dust only those nations who have abused the gifts and privileges of nature, and who, when arriving at the height of prosperity and power, have disregarded and despised those principles of morality and religion which form the true base of all society. How all the noble aspirations may be crushed and the instincts perverted ; how from a species of voluntary insanity, by our own fierce passions, and by a strange desire of mutual destruction, men rush on to contest and to ruin, is well illustrated by the past of the slave faction.

XII

It is evident that the black man has not deteriorated during his sojourn in these countries; on the contrary, he has improved in physique: the repulsive Congo type has changed, and the Circassian features appear. It is the result of the law of contact and example; it is the effect of civilization.

Has the white man gained in similar ratio? Go to the cotton fields and rice lands, and learn a lesson from the instructive contrast of the gaunt and apathetic white laborer, with the sturdy, well-developed, lively black. You will then observe that these vast alluvial lands, which rank in richness and fertility with the best on the globe, must be consigned to waste by reason of insalubrity, if not cultivated by races of men who are congenial to the soil and climate. There is no white race who can cultivate these lands, and enjoy life and establish society with any duration. Malaria would forbid, if other conditions were favorable.

The littoral lands of the lower tier of Slave States, which are composed of post tertiary and alluvial soils, tertiary sands and secondary chalk marls, can be tilled in safety and with economy and with gain only by the black man. Below the upper terraces and the slopes of the mountain ranges of the northern limits of these States, where we find the primary and metamorphic rocks and their debris, the white laborer cannot descend without contending with the full force of his nature, with disease, degeneration, and premature death.

There are now in the States of Florida, Alabama, Mississippi, and Louisiana thirty millions of acres of arable land yet belonging to the United States, unsold and unoccupied. In all England there are but seven million acres of uncultivated land.

XIII.

Malaria, that curse of the Circassian race, which is the chief source of the inefficiency and mortality of their efforts of colonizations in semi-tropical climes, exerts but little influence upon the negroes, and hence they are admirably qualified for the occupation of pestilential soils.

It appears from the statistics of the English that remittent and intermittent fevers, which prove the great source of inefficiency and mortality among the white troops in tropical climes, exert comparatively but little influence upon the blacks.

The writer has observed the fatal effects of the pernicious fevers upon the white inhabitants of the low coasts of Georgia and South Carolina, and has seen men perish in a single night from the deadly action of the miasms, whilst the negroes were unaffected.

During the English expedition up the Nile nearly all the whites were prostrated by fevers, and none of the native blacks were affected. After the French landed at Vera Cruz the yellow fever found great numbers of victims among the Europeans; but according to the report of the inspector-general, Regnaud, not one of the 600 negro soldiers and sailors from the West Indies, though hard at work there, were attacked, or rather not one of them died. There are hundreds of similar examples to illustrate the theory.

We cannot escape the mephitism of the soil. So long as we respire the air, so long shall we receive into the system the deleterious vapors by the respiratory apparatus, which is the most perfect of the absorbing agents: the time of effect is determined only by the health, the strength, and vigor of our forces. The destroying elements may take effect at once, or they may be resisted for a long, though definite period of time. Malaria alone has a wide range among the causes of human misery, and it is believed to cause more than half of the mortality of the human families on the globe.

Its deadly action, in depopulating cities and provinces, is well attested in history, and its effect upon the intellectual expansion is still more marked; sadness, languor, paludal cachexia, scrofulous, deformed, and short-lived offspring, are among its train of evils. In the Roman states alone, sixty thousand perish every year from this paludal influence. These deltas of the Southern States are among the greater miasmatic foyers of the world, and are as deadly in their miasms as the Campagna of Italy or the Sunderbunds of Hindostan.

XIV.

There are many reasons to induce the belief, that if properly directed, the blacks may attain distinction in social life and progress, and a higher degree of perfection in physical development. The skeleton of the negro is firmer and heavier, the bones being larger and thicker than that of any other race; but physiologists observe that the muscular development does not correspond to the strong dimensions of the frame. This deficiency of nature may be explained by the want of proper nutrition, or to physical causes within human control, for all proportions in nature are harmonious. Two of the most admirable boxers that have appeared in the British arena were blacks, and the dark, swarthy hue of the famous wrestler, Marseilles, reminds how common is the tinge of African blood in South France, Spain, and Italy.

While statistics appear to exhibit the physical superiority of the blacks in the low countries, they also prove how prone to pulmonary disease are they when migrating to the uplands, or higher latitudes, and how fearful the mortality. Thus Nature, it seems, offers serious barriers to their progress, and boundaries within which they must confine themselves or perish.

XV.

It has been urged that the intermingling of the freed blacks with the whites in these States will produce a variety of people more vicious, and less willing to be controlled by the social laws, than either pure race.

Of this there is but little danger, as ethnology will show. There will not be, under any ordinary circumstances, any intermingling of the two races, for the law of ethnic repugnance is too great. The strong ethnic antipathies will keep them apart. The possibility of the intermixture of families and races so widely remote is as rigidly limited as the law of chemical proportions, and the absorption of the minor quantity is inevitable. Give both races the same field for expansion in these States, and the white race will soon find itself in the minority, both of numbers and in physical strength; for, according to natural laws, the stronger blood always absorbs the weaker when there is unobstructed action, and especially when climate favors vastly one of the contending types.

There are to-day four or five times as many centenarians among the blacks as there are among the whites of the cotton regions.

In consideration of this subject of miscegenation, let us review the phenomena that have been brought to light by the naturalists who have studied hybridity among animals, and recall a few facts from history to support the experimentalists.

XVI.

In the animal world, in the wild state, hybrids are rarely if ever produced, and it is only from the experiments of the naturalists that the law of hybridity has been explained.

We see the bipartites appear, when two kindred species mix together under the influence of man, these animals partaking of the qualities of both. The horse and the ass; the ass, zebra, and hermione; the wolf and the dog; the dog and the jackal; the goat and the ram; the deer and the axis, &c., unite and breed; but these artificial species are not durable, and they have only limited fecundity. " The mongrels of the dog and the wolf are sterile from the third generation. The mongrels of the jackal and the dog are so from the fourth. Moreover, if we unite these mongrels to one of the two primitive species, they soon revert completely and totally to that species.

" The mongrel of the dog and jackal contains more of the jackal than the dog. It has the straight ears, the pendent tail; it does not bark; it is wild. It is more jackal than dog. This is the first product of the crossed union of the dog with the jackal. I continue to unite the successive produce, from generation to generation, with one of the two primitive roots, — with that of the dog, for example.

" The mongrel of the second generation does not bark yet, but it has the ears pendent at the tip: it is less wild.

" The mongrel of the third generation barks: it has pendent ears, raised tail: it is no longer wild. The mongrel of the fourth generation is entirely dog. Four generations, then, have sufficed to restore one of the two primitive types — the dog type; and four generations suffice also to restore the other type — the jackal type. Thus, when the mongrels produced from the union of two distinct species unite together, either become soon sterile, or they unite with one of the two primitive stocks, and they soon revert to this stock; in no case do they yield what may be called a new species, that is, an intermediate, durable species.

" Whether, then, we consider the external causes, — the succession of time, years, ages, revolutions of the globe, or internal causes, — that is to say, the crossing of the species, the species do not alter, do not change, nor pass from one

,to the other; the species is fixed." Such are the conclusions of the admirable efforts of Flourens.

" The imprint of each species," says Buffon, " is a type,
the principal features of which are engraved in characters
ineffaceable, and permanent forever; but all the accessory
touches vary; no individual perfectly resembles another."

XVII.

Among the human families, the law of hybridity, which
has been pointed out so clearly by Flourens, has also its
fixed and inflexible rules; these rules have not been so
well studied with men as with animals, but it is believed
to have its limit at the seventh generation. At all events,
the experiments of human hybridism, and acclimation in
strange latitudes, have always in time ended in disaster;
and that such will always be the fate of the attempted
union of different races in unfavorable climes, have been
the views of Humboldt, of Canning, of Guizot, and other
profound statesmen. We observe among the races in
savage life a natural repugnance to unite: as for instance,
the negroes and the fairer people of the Philippine and
Polynesian Isles show no disposition to unite; and though
living side by side, in the same country, for a long period,
they have not produced an intermediate race. Neither
do the Eskimos nor the Red Men, neither do the Caffres
nor the Hottentots mix, for in the state of nature the law
of ethnic repugnance is supreme. It is only in the artificial and depraved states of society that hybrids appear,
and their existence is of short and fixed duration.

The apparent duration and perfection of the Coulouglis,

the bipartates of the Bergers and Turks, may be an exception to the general rule.   But the results of the mingling
of human families, widely separated, is generally very
decided.

The Creoles, produced by the African with the Span-
iard, Italian, and the Southern French, possess considerable durability, but disease and degeneration soon appear
when the black mingles with the blood and humors of
the more northern nations.   With all these mixtures there
is a profound characteristic, which constitutes the unity,
identity, and reality of the species, which is, continuous
fecundity ;   and this characteristic never varies : it is immutable.   The mulattoes live less time than the black
or the white race, and their offspring perish readily, and
are rarely prolific, except when united with stronger individuals of either primitive type, to which they soon
return.

XVIII.

The blacks have been too degraded to more than conceive of liberty, too debased to think of resistance to the
forces that crushed them, and they have neither observed,
nor sought for opportunities, to throw off their chains and
sweep over the lands, like a destroying element, with the
accumulated wrongs of centuries.   Yet there were black
men among them who were capable of high cultivation.
The long contact with the superior white race had recast
the faculties of their mind, and had altered perceptibly the
rugged contour of their forms and features.

The writer observed with wonder in the regiment of
black men which formed part of the column of the des-

perate assault upon Fort Wagner, beautiful heads, whose classic and regular outlines recalled the finest of the antique.

We believe with the writer in the " Revue des Deux Mondes," that contact with the white races has given the negro the lines of the Caucasian form, and that the Congo type can disappear or become greatly modified.

These changes in the typical form, which we have since observed elsewhere, appear to have taken place sometimes without the admixture of the blood of the whites.

That the black men in the United States army fought well, no one will deny; that they conducted themselves admirably in the murderous assaults at Fort Wagner, or under the destroying fire at Olustee, and in many other conflicts, every one possessed of any candor will admit. When we consider the degradation whence they suddenly rose, and the steadiness and firmness, and the manly bearing they exhibited after the few lessons of military training, we are compelled to render thanks to them for their efforts in the struggle for national existence, and to admit the probability of their attaining that degree of intelligence, wisdom, and virtue which distinguish the true citizen. That these men will attain the standard of intellect of the Caucasian, we neither expect nor believe; but we do maintain, that in the nature of every race, however debased by prejudice, and the avarice of superior society, there exists the element of honesty, virtue, truth, and a horror of wrong, which may be developed and turned to the good of all society, in repelling and resisting the force of machination, the intrigue which arises from disappointed ambition, or the insatiable lust of more favored and less considerate classes.

No one acquainted with the history of the commerce of human beings will wonder at the present condition of the blacks, or that they have not risen in the scale of social and intellectual advancement. For, looking back to the primitive ages we may see how the human species have been depressed in servitude, and how the very same families, who carried the arts and sciences to celestial limits, were affected by this influence. Persons of the same blood and inheritance as the best families of Greece and Rome, were often reduced to slavery, and they sank rapidly under its debasing effects. They were tamed like the black man of the South; "like brutes, by the stings of hunger and the lash; and their education was so conducted as to render them commodious instruments of labor for their possessors. This degradation of course depressed their minds, restricted the expansion of their faculties, stifled almost every effort of genius, and exhibited them to the world as beings endued with inferior capacities to the rest of mankind. But for this opinion there appears to have been no foundation in truth or justice. Equal to their fellow-men in natural talents, and alike capable of improvement, any apparent or real difference between them and some others must have been owing to the mode of education, to the rank they were doomed to occupy, and to the treatment they were appointed to endure."

After all, the world appears to be a vast arena, where the good and the bad are gathered together, and men are left to their own efforts, whether to rise up in that scale of intelligence and virtue which conducts to immortality, or to grovel deeper into the depths of degradation, where there is nothing but death and annihilation. The vault of heaven grows in immensity as we gaze into its limitless expanse, whilst the shadows and attractions of earth fade away from view, or allure only those who have forsaken nature.

XVIII.

Have the European races advanced in these latitudes in strength of mind and body with equal ratio as the black man? We think not. Let us consider.

The qualities of plants and vegetables are often affected by external influences, so as to assume different characters, and the impressions upon the leaves and the fruits are distinctly marked. These alterations, degenerations, and modifications may disguise the primitive type so far that it is no longer recognizable. We observe these properties among all organic bodies, among those of the animal and as well as of the vegetable world. The vine and its golden extracts are very much dependent upon these influences.

The exquisite bouquet, the soul-inspiring qualities of the best varieties of wine, cannot be acquired by the efforts of man at pleasure; without the generous nature of the soil, the rays of sunlight, and the inspiring breezes of favored localities and climes, the extract of the pressed grape is without that flavor and force which warm into life the brilliancy of the imagination, the nobility of the soul.

There is also a marked effect of soil and climate upon

the odor of plants, and in their narcotic constituents. Does not the same law affect man?

The Italian violets grow sweeter as we climb the Alpine slopes ; the mignonette blooms with greater perfection and perfume as we approach the shores of the lowlands of the Mediterranean. We find the finest types of the human race among the uplands and the mountains ; below, on the low coasts and river margins, where pestilences are generated, the physical and mental forces do not fully expand, and we find there neither liberty, virtue, nor science.

Dr. Rusdorf, in his work on the influence of European climate, regards the temperate zone as the brain-making region, and attempts to prove it by physiological deductions. The brain of the Caucasian, he says, determines the superiority over the other races, and it is the standard of the organism. This, he maintains, is produced by the richness of albumen in the blood, which is also dependent upon the oxygen of pure air. The extensive observations of the English Registrar-General show indisputably that the elevation of the soil exercises as decided an influence on the English race as it does on the native races of other climes and soils. They also show that the finest animals are raised in the healthiest districts. We see that certain heights above the plains are remarkably exempt from maladies which devastate nations inhabiting lower levels. Cholera, remittent fever, yellow fever, and plague, disappear at well-defined degrees of elevation.

At Vera Cruz, and along its latitude, the yellow fever vanishes at the height of three thousand feet above the Gulf shores.

The Prussian, in his "Medicinische Geographie," appears to indicate with great degree of certainty the limits and altitudes of the three zones, into which he classifies the catarrhal, the dysenteric, and the scrofulous diseases. The scrofulous zone ceases at an altitude of two thousand feet above the level of the sea, and here, he says, there is no pulmonary consumption, scrofula, cancer, or typhus fever. "It is," says Babinet, "the climate of each country which permits or arrests the development of the human race, which, joined with the industry of populations, imposes limits to the numerical force of each meteorological district, and which subsists four million of men in fertile Belgium, which is no more than a small fraction of the territory of France, whilst Siberia can with difficulty nourish a part of that number with an extent which is twenty-six times that of France." "All over the world, physical circumstances," exclaims Draper, "control the human race."

XIX.

It is vain to assert that the atmospheres of the maritime or the low levels do not affect the physical and mental condition of men; and after all, Fontenelle was right when he maintained, in a curious paradox, that inspiration is a barometer that varies, which mounts to genius or descends to absurdity, according to the inconstancy of the weather; that there are unhealthy countries, full of mists, winds, tempests, that never produce clear understandings; and, on the contrary, there are lands with beautiful skies and fields filled with sunlight and roses which give out flashes of divine light.

Nearly all of the Grecian lyrists were born in the enchanting climates, and among the beautiful scenes of the Asiatic shore or the isles of the Ægean Sea. Most of the eminent men of Italy rose from similar inspirations, which Michael Angelo observed when speaking of Vasari in terms of admiration. Historians say that the sun was never softer, the heavens brighter, the roses more prolific, the winds more perfumed, than in the dawn of the eighteenth century, which produced that "wild garland of beautiful women who recalled by their graces, their genius, the courtesans of Greece," which gave birth to those philosophers who gave a new impetus to liberty and religion.

XX.

According to some writers, the unequal distribution of solar heat over the earth is the cause of marked differences in national character ; others refer the distinctive effects to the quality of the air they breathe. Arbuthnot maintains that air not only fashions the body, but has also had great influence in forming language ; that the close, serrated method of speaking of Northern nations was due to coldness of the climate, and hesitation of opening the mouth ; whilst the sweet, sonorous phrases of temperate climes, like those of the Mediterranean, were due to the mildness of climate, where the vocal organs could be exposed without danger. " It is incontestable," also writes Alfred Maury, in his " Earth and Man," " that climate has upon the mode of government a considerable influence, because it exercises an immediate effect upon the character of individuals. In the warm countries, under an enervating atmosphere, where all inclines to effeminacy and idleness, the soul has not that energy and that force of will necessary to a people who wish to be free. Under a severe and cold climate, to the contrary, the character acquires more of energy, and the body more of activity. The passions are less violent, and leave to the reason a freer exercise. In the hot climes the instincts are impetuous, and they pass from an extreme of dejection to a state of exaltation which produces revolutions, insurrections, but which do not establish the independence. For, to the contrary, these violent crises introduce retaliation; and in the sanguinary conflicts, the power of an individual, although tyrannical, appears as a benefit, or is accepted as a necessity."

XXI.

The anger of the European has always raged with undefinable fury, when once aroused, in these southern latitudes, and especially in the regions in question. The spirit is the same, whether we review the cruel and useless extermination of the Indians in Cuba or Florida; the massacres of the Mexicans by the merciless Spaniards; the internecine slaughter of the French, English, and Spaniards along the coasts of South Carolina, Georgia, and Florida; the extermination of whole tribes, like the Yemassee, or the forced removal of the red men from the broad lands of their birthplace and inheritance. All show the implacable depth of his avarice or his ire. It was not merely the honor of subjugation, of conquering strange races, that was the object of the politics, and that excited the emulation of these iron-mailed and iron-hearted men and their descendants: it seems to have been an irresistible desire to immolate human races, to glut with blood that thirst for destruction which arises from depraved and burning hearts.

It was the same spirit, under the mask of avarice, that tore the well-behaved Creeks and Cherokees from the homes of their ancestors, and banished them to the prairies of the West; that hunted down the last Seminole in the everglades of Florida, where there are to-day twenty millions of acres of land unsold and unoccupied.

It was the same spirit that, in later times, recklessly and ruthlessly destroyed, at Camp Sumter, an army of freemen, under the pretence of treating them as prisoners of war.

XXII.

Yet this depraved fury does not appear to have been natural to the soil, climate, or the native races, as observed by the early navigators; although Ponce de Leon received his death-wound from them when he sought the fountain of youth in the everglades of Florida, and De Soto encountered fierce opposition from the red men of the forest when he pursued his way towards the Appalachian mountains in search of the mines of gold. But nevertheless the Europeans were treated almost always with kindness whenever they approached the Indian with good intentions.

Contrast the present time and the people with the period and the natives when the great Navigator discovered the adjacent isles. "Nature is here," he exclaims, "so pro-

lific, that property has not produced the feelings of avarice or cupidity.   These people seem to live in a golden
age, happy and quiet, amid open and endless gardens,
neither surrounded by ditches, divided by fences, nor protected by walls.   They behave honorably towards one
another, without laws, without books, without judges.
They consider him wicked who takes delight in harming another.   This aversion of the good to the bad seems
to be all their legislation."

These people with natural sentiments have passed
away, and new races, with strange and repulsive ideas,
have taken their place.   " Like the statue of Glaucus,
that time, the sea, the storms have so disfigured that it
resembles less a god than a ferocious beast, the human
soul, altered in the bosom of society by a thousand causes
rising without cessation, by the acquisition of a multitude
of creeds and errors, by the changes produced in the constitution of bodies by the continual shock of passions, has
caused a change in appearance almost unrecognizable ;
and we sooner find, instead of the being acting always by
certain and invariable principles, instead of that celestial
and majestic simplicity in which the Creator has left his
impress, the deformed contrast of the understanding in
delirium, and of the passion which pretends to reason."

XXIII.

Wherever society forms and sustains itself, there must
be adopted certain rules and laws to maintain it.

These seemingly arbitrary laws represent the interests,
the passions, and opinions of those who establish them,

10 *

and they differ widely, according to the nature of the men and the climate which they inhabit.

The inhabitants of hot climes and the cold zones present strange contrasts in their natural ideas of justice, as well as in instincts and appetites. The Turk regards intemperance as a crime, and polygamy as a virtue. The Englishman looks upon the one with complaisance, but regards the other with horror. Thus reason yields to physical force, or to the differences of climate; and what men call virtue in one clime, loses its force and beauty in another. Yet there are natural laws older than the empires of force or reason; more ancient than society itself; more powerful and sublime than the passions and interests of men. These laws of kindness, of mercy, of friendship, like elementary language, come from divination.

Nature has planted certain instincts in the bosoms of all the different races of the globe alike; and these become developed according to cultivation, or debased according to degrading influences. The good of society may define the measure between good and evil, but it cannot extinguish the principles, or obliterate the sharply defined distinctions. The will of the Creator has manifested itself clearly in the workings of the natural world, if it has not been revealed to us in those tablets which fell from the skies.

XXIV.

The benign influences of society, the exercise of politeness and reason, inspire polished and agreeable manners; yet, in the midst of these, we find men who think barbarity to be one of their rights; and they abuse their fellow-creatures without pretext, and commit murder without necessity, which is a degree of ferocity below that of the carnivorous animals; for they destroy life only when impelled by the motives of hunger. Societies of men are institutions of nature, and they are founded upon the principies of mutual obligations. Society relapses into barbarism when the golden rule of " doing as we would be done by " is violated; when individual liberty is lost; and when man treats his fellow-man as property under the right of force, and therefore without legal relations. Constitutions are the indices of the education and the aspiration of nations, and they keep pace with the onward march of intelligence. These become altered and modified, as the intellect and hearts of men expand; and it is nothing but bigotry that believes in the inviolability, the perfection of the doctrines and tenets of men in the present or the past. The wise man, says the old proverb, often changes his opinion, the fool never.

XXV.

Slavery appears to be coeval with war; and war is as ancient as the human race. Plutarch believed that there had been a time, a golden age, when there were neither masters nor slaves. The human mind, at the time when Plutarch wrote, was almost controlled by the empire of force. The selfishness and superstition of society fettered the nobility of nature, and healthy reason could not assume its rightful sway.

The depth of the philosophical reasoning, the degree of humanity of one of the brighest periods of antiquity, may be comprehended from the "Politics" of Aristotle, when he says, "To the Greeks belongs dominion over the barbarians, because the former have the understanding requisite to rule, the latter, the body only to obey. For the slave, considered simply as such, no friendship can be be entertained, but it may be felt for him, as he is a man." Some of the ancient nations, the most enthusiastic in the dreams of liberty, were the most savage and stern in their laws concerning their slaves; and they adhered to their brutal doctrines in defiance of nature with singular tenacity. The right of life and death over the slave was one of the fundamental principles of the society of the Athenians, Lacedemonians, Romans, and Carthaginians.

Strange condition of society among men who cultivated the arts and sciences so successfully! Yet it does not appear that any legislator attempted to abrogate servitude.

Stranger still that the glorious period of the reign of democracy at Athens should not have brought with it the universal freedom of men, when liberty was the divine ideal of its aspirations.

XXVI.

Not until the star of Christianity rose above the horizon of the pagan and superstitious world, softening the hearts of men and revealing to them a new life, did Slavery vanish from among refined and generous societies, under the charter, *Pro amore Dei, pro mercede animæ.* And never has it reappeared, except among those nations who have become debased from avarice, or depraved by ambition. When cupidity allows fanaticism to blind the mind with the belief that savages or negroes can be more easily converted to Christianity whilst in slavery than in freedom, then there is an end to social progress. Yet such were the ideas of Louis XIII. when he consigned the negroes of his colonies to Slavery. And such has been the creed of the slaveholders and breeders of America. The monstrous doctrine imposed itself upon the understandings of the slave faction, as the superstitions of the false prophets have fettered and crushed the minds of the pagan nations. It has debased their natural sentiments, as well as it has depressed and perverted their natural talents and virtues. " In the same manner," said Longinus, " as some children always remain pygmies, whose infant limbs, fettered by the prejudices and habits of servitude, are unable to expand themselves, or to attain that well-proportioned greatness which we admire in the ancients, who, living under a popular government, wrote with the same freedom as they acted."

XXVII.

We may learn from the history of the past, if we will not accept the data of the present, how climate, food, domesticity, or recognized customs of society may alter the minds and dispositions of men ; how they may gradually build up governments, founded upon monstrous ideas, and yet in unison with the compunctions of their conscience. Ascribe the origin to any cause you will, it does not alter the revolting facts, nor lessen the repulsiveness of the absurdity, nor the enormity of the crime. Volney believed " that the social institutions called

Government and Religion were the true sources and regulators of the activity or indolence of individuals and nations; that they were the efficient causes which, as they extend or limit the natural or superfluous wants, limit or extend the activity of all men. A proof that their influence operates in spite of the difference of climate and soil is, that Tyre, Carthage, and Alexandria formerly possessed the same industry as London, Paris, and Amsterdam; that the Buccaneers and the Malayans have displayed equal turbulence and courage with the Normans, and that the Russians and Polanders have the apathy and indifference of the Hindoos and the Negroes. But, as civil and religious institutions are perpetually varied and changed by the passions of men, their influence changes and varies in very short intervals of time. Hence it is that the Romans commanded by Scipio resembled so little those governed by Tiberius, and that the Greeks of the age of Aristides and Themistocles were so unlike those of the time of Constantine."

Volney observes that "the moral character of nations, taken from that of individuals, chiefly depends on the social state in which they live; since it is true that our actions are governed by our civil and religious laws, and since our habits are no more than a repetition of those actions, and our character only the disposition to act in such a manner under such circumstances, it evidently follows that these must essentially depend on the nature of the government and religion."

Says Addison, "In all despotic governments, though a particular prince may favor arts and letters, there is a natural degeneracy of mankind, as you may observe from

Augustus's reign, how the Romans lost themselves by degrees, until they fell to an equality with the most barbarous nations that surrounded them. Look upon Greece under its free states, and you would think its inhabitants lived in different climates and under different heavens from those at present, so different are the geniuses which are formed under Turkish slavery and Grecian liberty.

" Besides poverty and want, there are other reasons that debase the minds of men who live under Slavery, though I look on this as the principal. The natural tendency of despotic powers to ignorance and barbarity, though not insisted upon by others, is, I think, an unanswerable argument against that form of government, as it shows how repugnant it is to the good of mankind and the perfection of human nature, which ought to be the great end of all civil institutions."

" Liberty should reach every individual of a people, as they all share one common nature; if it only spreads among particular branches there had better be none at all, since such a liberty only aggravates the misfortune of those who are deprived of it, by setting before them a disagreeable subject of comparison."

" The pride of Athens," writes Mirabeau, " and the jealousy of the Greeks, banished forever the liberty of those countries, so long fortunate."

Such is and always was our world, covered from time to time with conquerors and slaves, because the conquering, in forging the irons of the unhappy, with which they bound them, sharpen those which must bind them in turn.

Such is and always will be man, from time to time despot

and slave, for man, denaturalized by servitude, becomes readily the most ferocious of animals if he escapes an instant from oppression. There is but one step from the despot to the slave, from the slave to the despot, and the chain becomes them alike.

XXVIII.

There are strange forces constantly at work: civilizations spring up, disappear, and sometimes, but rarely, return again after a sleep of ages: it seems as though genius laid fallow for a period, like the golden grains.

The Greek mind teaches the Arabs under the Caliphs of Bagdad and Cordova, and in turn the Arabian influence instructs the reviving European mind after the dark ages. The fall of Constantinople crushed the Greek mind completely. The genius and the "godlike men" of Rome vanished under the influence of the strong blood of the Goths, and the flourishing nations of the African shore have yielded so completely to physical and moral causes, that we justly doubt the story of their magnificence, their power, their intelligence.

We see the effete races infused with the fresh blood; the vigorous juices of the Scandinavians march forward with unparalleled pace to the triumphs of reason and philosophy. The pure, warm, healthy vitality of the North recalls to life the exact sciences, the laws of reasoning, and philosophy, and æsthetics, which, arising from Grecian genius, had slumbered for a thousand years.

XXIX.

In the slave lands of America a high order of intellect was proclaimed; but when analysis approached, it sank into mediocrity, or vanished into dust, like the forms in the ancient tombs when exposed to the light of heaven. Slavery has produced nothing but horror. The flashes of light that have burst forth through its mists have been the expiring efforts of genius. Here the sciences have always languished and declined to take root, for they are the offspring of genius and reason. The arts never appeared, for the spirit of imitation never arose. To cultivate the sciences, there is need of exalted desire, which comes from healthy and prosperous races or from celestial fire. Here there was the barbarity of ignorance; the only desires were to increase the enormities of their crimes, by the spread and general adoption of Slavery, and to conceal its proportions and influences beneath a cloud of mental darkness, which is frightful to contemplate, when placed in comparison with intelligent communities like New England, Belgium, and Prussia.

They thought to perpetuate an aristocratic power, and transmit the inheritance of Slavery as a blessing, but they forgot that in the formation of happy nations and states humanity forms the broad base; they forgot that ambitious and avaricious families quickly degenerate and disappear completely from the earth. The vicissitudes of political life hasten that decline which is commenced by riches and rank, when supported by morbid ideas and sentiments.

The noble families of Athens and Corinth, the patrician

body at Rome, vanished so rapidly as to excite the surprise of the nations they governed. The names of the descendants of the founders of Venice, written in the Libro di Oro, are no longer to be found among the living in Italy.

The same law is silently at work in our times.

XXX.

The inequalities of the earth's surface are like the rugosities of the human brain: the depths of the one contain the richest and most inexhaustible treasures of mineral wealth, as the wrinkles of the other collect the stores of mental lore. As the surface of the brain becomes less marked and rugged, the strength and scope of the mind vanish, and approach the standard of the lower animals; and likewise, as the elevated lands of the earth shrink in form, and sink into the level of the plain, so the characters of the races who inhabit them lose force and elevation.

Sometimes the minds of men are the reflections of the beauties and sublimities of nature. Sometimes men become degraded, and nature then does not inspire.

XXXI.

The lofty and diversified mountain range, or system of ranges, known as the Appalachian or Alleghany, rises or reappears in the State of New York, midway between the Atlantic coast and the shores of those fresh-water seas, Erie and Ontario. It then stretches down south-

westward, with its adjacent spurs, through the great
States of Pennsylvania and Virginia; then, dividing, it
forms, with its eastern range, the western and northern
limit of North and South Carolina and Georgia; and
with the western it intersects Tennessee, forming that
beautiful basin known among the white men as East Tennessee, but among the traditions of the red men as the
Garden of the Manitou — their God. In Northern Alabama, the separated ranges seemingly unite; and passing
southward, towards the central portion of the State, the
mountain summits gradually contract, and finally sink into
the level of the great alluvial plains, which stretch away,
without undulation, to the shores of the Gulf. These
huge masses of rock, dislocated and elevated like the
Vosges and the Hartz Mountains at the close of the car-
boniferous or devonian period of the earth's age, contain,
with the adjacent and connecting bands, — which are composed of the silurian, primitive, and metamorphic ledges,
— most of the accessible mineral wealth of the republic.
And the collective beds of iron, coal, marble, zinc, cop-
per, and gold are unsurpassed in similar extent and richness by the mines of any country of the known world,
with the exception of those wonderful deposits of ores and
minerals among the unexplored and almost inaccessible
recesses and plateaus of the Sierra Nevada or the Andes.

With the exception of the northern extremity of this
mountain group, these mines of natural wealth may be
said to have been unexplored. Below the rich and popu-
lous State of Pennsylvania, the hum of human industry
ceases; for we then pass into the paralyzing shadow of
Slavery. This Slavery forbade the development of the

earth's treasures, as well as the enlightenment of the minds of the poor and ignorant whites. The forges of Vulcan would have hammered out and broken into fragments the chains of that bondage which not only oppressed the fettered blacks, but debased, with its corroding influence, the competing labor of the white man.

The slaveholders concealed this immense natural wealth from the eyes of science from motives of policy; and rather than incur the hazard of revolution, by educating the masses of their own people, they preferred to neglect their natural advantages, and to send to distant and even foreign lands the products of their fields and their system, to be worked up into the marvellous fabrics of human ingenuity and skill. This same State of Virginia, which is the real gateway to the empires of the West, and which is not surpassed in natural physical advantages by any equal extent of territory on the globe, is the most ignorant of all of the States of the republic. Ninety thousand of its native-born free people, over twenty years of age, before the war could not read nor write; whilst sterile and stormy Maine, with her cold lands and colder skies, contained but two thousand of the same class, out of a population more than half as great. And New England, with a population of almost three times as great as the free people of Virginia, is ashamed by the number of seven thousand illiterate natives past the age of twenty. Who will wonder at the display of barbarity and audacity when the statistics of education and ignorance are exhibited? " Education and liberty," says Mirabeau, " are the bases of all social harmony and all human prosperity."

Which can civilization curse the most, London or Amsterdam? the Dutch who introduced Slavery, or the English who thought Virginia a good place to "colonize aristocratic stupidity," and who sent colonists, who were, according to the historian, "fitter to breed a riot than to found a colony." The condition of the present day shows how rigidly the first instructions have been observed and enforced. "Thank God," writes one of its early governors to the English Privy Council, "thank God there are no free schools or printing, and I hope we shall not have any these hundred years! for learning has brought disobedience and heresy and sects into the world, and printing has divulged them and libels against the best government. God keep us from both!"

XXXII.

And so these mines, and fields, and forests, remain to the present day, unsurveyed, unexplored and unknown, save to a few wanderers of science.

In Northern Alabama, where the terminating slopes of this upheaval of rocks disappear beneath the level of the vast cotton fields, which number their acres by the million, there appear enormous deposits of iron ore, of extraordinary richness and depth, lying in juxtaposition with corresponding beds of limestones and coal.

Here is alone sufficient material for the iron fingers and forges and the steam power to fabricate the vegetable growths, the harvests of the vast and fertile plains of the entire South, and to build up with enduring form those great and thriving cities which are seen in the dim vista of the future of the Mississippi Valley, with its hundred millions of people. These elevations, when denuded of their immense primeval forests of pine and oak, will be covered with constant verdure, affording sure sustenance to numberless flocks and herds of kine, which will require less care than the cattle of the plains of Texas or the pampas of Peru, since Nature, with her caverns and narrow valleys, will afford shelter from the destructive storms of winter and the chilling blasts of spring.

Between the two great spurs of the divided mountain range which encompass the head-waters and tributaries of the Tennessee, appears the garden spot of the Republic: the soils, enriched by the decomposition of the blue limestones, are here of great strength and endurance; the innumerable streams are of sufficient force and volume to satisfy the wants of industry and mechanics, whilst the lofty mountains, which rise to the height of seven thousand feet above the ocean, with their broad and impressive shadows, temper the atmospheres, so that the body can labor and the mind expand.

To the natural beauties of the landscape art has yet added nothing: from the teeming harvests of the valleys, from the massive ledges of minerals, man has yet detracted nothing.

Nature here is almost inexhaustible.

No wonder that the dying Indian returns to the region of the Hiwassee to end his days on earth, impelled by an irresistible desire to behold once more the wonders and beauties of natural scenery, which are preserved among the fading traditions of the tribes that have been banished to the far off western frontiers.

XXXIII.

From beneath the eastern aspect of the mountains of Alabama, a broad belt of metamorphic rocks bursts forth, and trends to the north-eastward, following the mountain ranges in almost parallel lines through the States of Georgia, South and North Carolina, and disappearing in Virginia beneath the waters of the Potomac. These lands of decomposed mica and talcose schists contain throughout their broad extent particles of gold; and some of the narrow and circumscribed fields are unsurpassed in their undeveloped richness by any of the known gold fields of similar extent in the world. These auriferous soils, owned or controlled by the slaveholder, have yielded, by the superficial scratchings and washings of the slave and the poor white, during the period since the discovery of the precious metal, about forty millions of dollars. There are not less than one hundred millions more within the reach and grasp of skilled and determined labor.

Along beside, and traversing through and through these golden rocks and sands, occur immense bands of itacolumite, known, from its flexibility, as the elastic sandstone. They stretch from Alabama to the interior of North Carolina, bursting forth now as great flexible bands of stone, and then bulging out as entire mountains. This singular formation is the same that has been recognized in Brazil, Ural Mountains, and Hindostan, as the matrix of the diamond; and here, nearly one hundred of the precious gems of fine water have been picked up from the earth, from time to time, by the careless observer.

XXXIV.

This upheaval of the earth's surface, reminding the geographer of the Italian peninsula, vaguely perhaps in form, in natural fertility and in purity of climate, is destined to play an important part in the future advancement of the Republic. For here is the heart of the eastern portion of the continent, geographically, climatologically, and mineralogically. Here Nature is too prolific to be long neglected by the cupidity or the ambition of men, when the barriers and obstructions of inquiry and settlement, which have been reared against the advance and design of civilization by the Slave Faction, shall have been removed. When the tide of European emigration, which steadily brings to the New World the pure blood and youth of races, turns its stream of industrial life towards these valleys, mountain slopes, and terraces; when the laws of alimentation are understood and properly observed; when the spire of the school-house rises in the vista of every landscape, or points the way at every cross-road, — then we may expect to see a new variety of the human race appear, possessed of remarkable physical strength and beauty, and whose ideas and efforts, typical of the healthy and developed mind, will, like the influences of New England and Scandinavia, give fresh impulse and impress to the civilizations of the earth.

XXXV.

Races of men — nations — even the lesser communities, during the periods of their social existence, erect monuments, or leave, unwillingly sometimes, traces of their progress, their advancement, their culture, as memorials for the admiration, or as the objects of horror for the contempt, of future generations.

The gigantic pyramids and sphinxes of Egypt tell of the civilization of their extinct founders; the airy and graceful columns, with the wonderful sculptures of the Parthenon, disclose the degree of the perfection and the delicacy of the Greek mind. Rome, though long since vanished from among the nations of the earth, has left the impress of her force, grandeur, and wisdom in those laws which now direct the tribunals of men; the lofty and colossal structures of the temples of the Rhine are the emblems of faith as well as the masterpieces of the Gothic heart and intellect; even the mysterious and history-forgotten Druids have left their rude reminiscences in those weird circles of enormous and cyclopean rocks, beyond which all is darkness.

Thus men perpetuate their memories among the annals of the earth. But after their long period of existence and progress, what have the Slave Faction left for the historian to contemplate with satisfaction? for an attentive world to study, imitate, and admire? What beyond this appalling cloud of ignorance have they left as legacy to the poor white? What besides misery, violence, and crime have they bequeathed to the black man? With what treasures, in the estimation of mankind, have they en-

riched themselves, or left as inheritance to their degenerate offspring?

The history of this remorseless party, its selfish and
sordid aims, its cruel results, will always find place among
the annals of civilized man so long as the noblest acts of
men are admired, and so long as the dark deeds of cruelty
appall and overshadow our better nature. Thermopylæ,
Marathon, and the holy sites where Liberty has struggled
for existence, and where men have risen above the tram-
mels of their earthly natures, will be remembered no
longer than this field of blood and torture among the
obscure forests of Georgia.

XXXVI.

Who will say that Nature and Liberty were the genii
who directed the labors of the leaders of the Rebellion?

Soil, climate, hereditary traditions, and customs of society, give to a people the fierceness and gentleness of
character, as well as the perfection of mind and body.
This fatal Stockade, with the silent mound of earth which
contains its harvest of death, is a fair and just exponent
of the bigoted and selfish policy that struck down the
Flag of the Republic; of that cruel and unearthly spirit
which has despised all the " attachments with which God
has formed the chain of human sympathies," and which,
without a tear of remorse, has strewn the Atlantic Ocean
with a broad pathway of human bones!

APPENDIX.

NOTES.

Since the close of the war, and since the time when the sketch of the graveyard was taken, Colonel Moore, of the U. S. Quartermaster's Department, has been to Andersonville, under orders from the Secretary of War, and arranged the cemetery in a very acceptable manner. All of the stakes were removed, and neat head-boards placed instead, with the names of the dead properly painted in black letters. The ground has been cleared up by this efficient officer, and the cemetery carefully laid out into walks, adorned with flowers and trees. Colonel Moore, in his report to the Quartermaster-General, writes the following account: —

"The dead were found buried in trenches, on a site selected by the rebels, about three hundred yards from the stockade. The trenches varied in length from fifty to one hundred and fifty yards. The bodies in the trenches were from two to three feet below the surface, and in several instances, where the rain had washed away the earth, but a few inches. Additional earth was, however, thrown upon the graves, making them of still greater depth. So close were they buried, without coffins, or the ordinary clothing to cover their nakedness, that not more than twelve inches were allowed to each man. Indeed, the little tablets marking their resting-places, measuring hardly ten inches in width, almost touch each other. United States soldiers, while prisoners at Andersonville, had been detailed to inter their companions; and by a simple stake at the head of each grave, which bore a number corresponding with a similarly numbered name upon the Andersonville hospital record, I was enabled to identify, and mark with a neat tablet, similar to those in the cemeteries at Washington, the number, name, rank, regiment, company, and date of death of twelve thousand four hundred and sixty-one graves; there being but four hundred and fifty-one that bore the sad inscription, 'Unknown U. S. Soldier.'"

Extract from letters of the rebel Senator Foote, dated Montreal, June 21, 1865.

"Touching the Congressional report referred to, I have this to say: A month or two anterior to the date of said report, I learned from a government officer of respectability, that the prisoners of war then confined in and about Richmond were suffering severely from want of provisions. He told me, further, that it was manifest to him that a systematic scheme was on foot for subjecting these unfortunate men to starvation; that the Commissary-General, Mr. Northrup (a most wicked and heartless wretch), had addressed a communication to Mr. Seddon, the Secretary of War, proposing to withhold meat altogether from military prisoners then in custody, and to give them nothing but bread and vegetables; and that Mr. Seddon had indorsed the document containing this communication affirmatively. I learned, further, that by calling upon Major Ould, the commissioner for exchange of prisoners, I would be able to obtain further information upon the subject. I went to Major Ould immediately, and obtained the desired information. Being utterly unwilling to countenance such barbarity for a moment, — regarding, indeed, the honor of the whole South as concerned in the affair, — I proceeded without delay to the hall of the House of Representatives, called the attention of that strangely constituted body to the subject, and insisted upon an immediate committee of investigation."

As to the capacity of the bakery, any one can make his own estimates from the plan given. The foreman of the government bakery at Nashville, gives his views in the following note : —

"Sir: Our system in wheaten flour bread is, five men bake six ovens full in the twelve hours; one oven full, 36 pans; 9 loaves (18 rations) in each pan; 36 pans $\times$ 18 = 648 $\times$ 6 ovens full = 3888 $\times$ 2 (for twenty-four hours) = 7776 rations : this is done by two ovens. Say six men on each oven (any more would be in the way), two and a half hours to knead and bake each oven full (almost impossible), ten ovens full in the twelve hours in the day time (two ovens five times full in the twelve hours), ten ovens full in the twelve hours in the night time, each oven full 40 pans, 12 rations in each (20 oz. of corn bread); 40 pans $\times$ 12 = 480 $\times$ 10 for day's work = 4800 + 4800 for night work = 9600 rations in the twenty-four hours.

Sir, all the above are in the extreme.   Most respectfully,

JOHN WITHERSPOON, Foreman U. S. Bakery."

The hospital register gives the following data as to the number of prisoners present during each month, the number treated medically, and the average number of deaths: —

Month.		Number of Prisoners.	Number in Hospital.	Average Daily Deaths.
February,	1864.	1,600	33	..
March,	"	4,603	909	9
April,	"	7,875	870	19
May,	"	13,486	1,190	23
June,	"	22,352	1,605	40
July,	"	28,689	2,156	56
August,	"	32,193	3,709	99
September.	"	17,733	3,026	89
October,	"	5,885	2,245	51
November,	"	2,024	242	16
December,	"	2,218	431	5
January,	1865.	4,931	595	6
February,	"	5,195	365	5
March,	"	4,800	140	3

The greatest number of deaths, on any single day, was on the 23d of August, 1864, and was 127, or one death every eleven minutes.

The fact of the employment of blood-hounds is too notorious to admit of doubt.   Many packs of dogs were kept, and a profitable business was done in the catching of escaped prisoners.   Ben Harris was seen to receive pay for the capture of sixty prisoners, at thirty dollars apiece.   That some of the pursued were killed in the forests during the pursuit, there is no doubt in the writer's mind, from the evidence offered.

The following table was collated from the hospital records of the prison, and is believed, by the writer and clerks who were employed at the rebel office, to be quite correct : —

Month.	Deaths in Hospital.	Deaths in Stockade.	Deaths in Small Pox Hospital.	Total.
February, 1864. .	1	..	..	1
March, " . .	262	15	5	282
April, " . .	471	71	34	576
May, " . .	633	65	10	708
June, " . .	1,041	150	10	1,201
July, " . .	1,119	614	5	1,738
August, " . .	1,489	1,592	..	3,081
September, " . .	1,255	1,423	..	2,678
October, " . .	1,294	301	..	1,595
November, " . .	494	..	..	494
December, " . .	166	2	..	168
January, 1865. .	191	8	..	199
February, " . .	147	..	..	147·
March, " . .	100	..	..	100
Total.	8,663	4,241	64	12,968
Hung in stockade for crime.				6
Total deaths as registered.				12,974

The hospital records show that 17,873 patients were registered, and that 823 of these were exchanged, and about 25 took the oath of allegiance, leaving 17,048 to be accounted for, giving a mortality of seventy-six per cent. Besides the registered dead, there were some who perished by the falling of the excavations in the stockade, and others destroyed by hounds and hunters in the forests.

The meteorological tables and the vegetal charts of Blodgett will give the rain-fall of this region in comparison with the other districts of the United States.

The following table, which was compiled by the author from the official records of the British army, gives the number of soldiers who were killed in action, or afterwards perished from their wounds, in many of the great battles of the British empire : —

Year.	Battles.	Total Strength engaged.	Estimated Deaths.
1809.	Talavera,	22,100	1,445
1811.	Albuera,	9,000	1,358
1812.	Salamanca,	30,500	770
1813.	Vittoria,	42,000	890
1815.	Ligny,	...	..
..	Quatre Bras,	...	..
..	Wavre,	49,900	3,245
..	Waterloo,	...	..
..	New Orleans,	6,000	625
1854.	Crimea,	...	4,595
Total number of deaths from wounds. . . .			12,928

STATISTICS FROM THE CENSUS REPORTS OF 1860.
GEORGIA.

Counties.	Corn, bushels.	Wheat, bushels.	Cotton, bales.	Potatoes, bushels.	Peas and Beans, bush.
Macon. . .	313,906	22,312	10,248	86,000	37,836
Lee. . . .	319,653	2,250	14,445	60,000	34,599
Sumter. .	386,892	8,396	14,423	92,234	12,483
Dougherty.	356,812	553	9,580	56,310	23,061
Total. .	1,377,263	33,511	48,696	294,544	108,019

Counties.	Land improved, acres.	Land unimproved, acres.	Number of Slaves.
Macon.	88,353	108,176	4,865
Lee.	85,840	113,172	4,947
Sumter.	102,327	160,742	4,890
Dougherty.	91,470	99,048	6,079
Total.	367,990	481,138	20,781

There were, in 1860, nearly 600,000 cattle and swine in the State of Florida alone, whilst Maine had but 200,000 at the same time. Georgia and Alabama had together, in 1860, 5,000,000 of cattle and swine, and they produced during the same year more than 60,000,000 bushels of corn, 4,000,000 bushels of wheat, and 13,000,000 bushels of potatoes. All New England, during the same period, produced but 1,000,000 bushels of wheat and 9,000,000 bushels of corn, although containing a million more people than Georgia and Alabama.

The following is a copy of the order relating to the treatment of the rebel prisoners in the hands of the United States authorities. Contrast it with the rebel barbarities.

A.

OFFICE OF COMMISSARY GENERAL OF PRISONERS,
WASHINGTON, April 20, 1864.

[Circular.]

By authority of the War Department, the following Regulations will be observed at all stations where prisoners of war and political or state prisoners are held. The Regulations will supersede those issued from this office July 7, 1861 : —

I. The Commanding Officer at each station is held accountable for the discipline and good order of his command, and for the security of the prisoners; and will take such measures, with the means placed at his disposal, as will best secure these results. He will divide the prisoners into companies, and will cause written reports to be made to him of their condition every morning, showing the changes made during the preceding twenty-four hours, giving the names of the "joined," "transferred," "deaths," &c. At the end of every month, Commanders will send to the Commissary General of Prisoners a Return of Prisoners, giving names and details to explain "alterations." If rolls of "joined" or "transferred" have been forwarded during the month, it will be sufficient to refer to them on the return, according to forms furnished.

II. On the arrival of any prisoners at any station, a careful comparison of them with the rolls which accompany them will be made, and all errors on the rolls will be corrected. When no roll accompanies the prisoners, one will immediately be made out, containing all the information required, as correct as can be, from the statements of prisoners themselves. When the prisoners are citizens, the town, county, and State from which they come will be given on the rolls, under the headings Rank, Regiment, and Company. At stations where prisoners are received frequently, and in small parties, a list will be furnished every fifth day — the last one in the month may be for six days — of all prisoners received during the preceding five days. Immediately on their arrival, prisoners will be required to give up all arms and weapons of every description, of which the Commanding Officer will require an accurate list to be made. When prisoners are forwarded for exchange, duplicate parole rolls, signed by the prisoners, will be sent with them, and an ordinary roll will be sent to the Commissary General of Prisoners. When they are transferred from one station to another, an ordinary roll will be sent with them, and a copy of it to the Commissary General of Prisoners. In all cases, the officer charged with conducting prisoners will report to the officer under whose order he acts the execution of his service, furnishing a receipt for the prisoners delivered, and accounting by name for those not delivered; which report will be forwarded, without delay, to the Commissary General of Prisoners.

III. The hospital will be under the immediate charge of the senior Medical Officer present, who will be held responsible to the Commanding Officer for its good order and the proper treatment of the sick. A fund for this hospital will be created, as for other hospitals. It will be kept separate from the fund of the hospital for the troops, and will be expended for the objects specified, and in the manner prescribed, in paragraph 1212, Revised Regulations for the Army of 1863, except that the requisition of the Medical Officer in charge, and the bill of purchase, before payment, shall be approved by the Commanding Officer. When this "fund" is sufficiently large, it may be expended also for shirts and drawers for the sick, the expense of washing clothes, articles for policing purposes, and all articles and

11 *

objects indispensably necessary to promote the sanitary condition of the hospital.

IV. Surgeons in charge of hospitals where there are prisoners of war will make to the Commissary General of Prisoners, through the Commanding Officer, semi-monthly reports of deaths, giving names, rank, regiment, and company; date and place of capture; date and cause of death; place of interment, and number of grave. Effects of deceased prisoners will be taken possession of by the Commanding Officer — the money and valuables to be reported to this office (see note on blank reports), the clothing of any value to be given to such prisoners as require it. Money left by deceased prisoners, or accruing from the sale of their effects, will be placed in the Prison Fund.

V. A fund, to be called "The Prison Fund," and to be applied in procuring such articles as may be necessary for the health and convenience of the prisoners, not expressly provided for by General Army Regulations, 1863, will be made by withholding from their rations such parts thereof as can be conveniently dispensed with. The Abstract of Issues to Prisoners, and Statement of the Prison Fund, shall be made out, commencing with the month of May, 1864, in the same manner as is prescribed for the Abstract of Issues to Hospital and Statement of the Hospital Fund (see paragraphs 1209, 1215, and 1246, and Form 5, Subsistence Department, Army Regulations, 1863), with such modifications in language as may be necessary. The ration for issue to prisoners will be composed as follows, viz. : —

Hard Bread, ...	{ 14 oz. per one ration, or
	{ 18 oz. Soft Bread one ration.
Corn Meal, ...	18 oz. per one ration.
Beef, ...	14 " " "
Bacon or Pork, . . .	10 " " "
Beans, ...	6 qts. per 100 men.
Hominy or Rice, . . .	8 lbs. " "
Sugar, ...	14 " " "
R. Coffee, ...	5 lbs. ground, or 7 lbs. raw, per 100 men.
Tea, ...	18 oz. per 100 men.
Soap, ...	4 " " "

Adamantine Candles, . . 5 Candles per 100 men.
Tallow Candles, . . . 6 " " "
Salt, ... 2 qts. " "
Molasses, ... 1 qt. " "
Potatoes, ... 30 lbs. " "

When beans are issued, hominy or rice will not be. If at any time it should seem advisable to make any change in this scale, the circumstances will be reported to the Commissary General of Prisoners for his consideration.

VI. Disbursements to be charged against the Prison Fund will be made by the Commissary of Subsistence, on the order of the Commanding Officer; and all such expenditures of funds will be accounted for by the Commissary, in the manner prescribed for the disbursements of the Hospital Fund. When in any month the items of expenditures on account of the Prison Fund cannot be conveniently entered on the Abstract of Issues to Prisoners, a list of the articles and quantities purchased, prices paid, statement of services rendered, &c., certified by the Commissary as correct, and approved by the Commanding Officer, will accompany the Abstract. In such cases it will only be necessary to enter on the Abstract of Issues the total amount of funds thus expended.

VII. At the end of each calendar month, the Commanding Officer will transmit to the Commissary General of Prisoners a copy of the "Statement of the Prison Fund," as shown in the Abstract of Issues for that month, with a copy of the list of expenditures specified in preceding paragraph, accompanied by vouchers, and will indorse thereon, or convey in letter of transmittal, such remarks as the matter may seem to require.

VIII. The Prison Fund is a credit with the Subsistence Department, and at the request of the Commissary General of Prisoners may be transferred by the Commissary General of Subsistence in the manner prescribed by existing Regulations for the transfer of Hospital Fund.

IX. With the Prison Fund may be purchased such articles, not provided for by regulations, as may be necessary for the health and

proper condition of the prisoners, such as table furniture, cooking
utensils, articles for policing, straw, the means for improving or enlarging the barracks or hospitals, &c.   It will also be used to pay clerks
and other employees engaged in labors connected with prisoners.   No
barracks or other structures will be erected or enlarged, and no alterations made, without first submitting a plan and estimate of the cos
to the Commissary General of Prisoners, to be laid before the Secretary of War for his approval; and in no case will the services of
clerks or of other employees be paid for without the sanction of the
Commissary General of Prisoners.   Soldiers employed with such
sanction will be allowed 40 cents per day when employed as clerks,
stewards, or mechanics; 25 cents a day when employed as laborers.

X. It is made the duty of the Quartermaster, or, when there is
none, the Commissary, under the orders of the Commanding Officer,
to procure all articles required, and to hire clerks or other employees.
All bills for service or for articles purchased will be certified by the
Quartermaster, and will be paid by the Commissary on the order of
the Commanding Officer, who is held responsible that all expenditures
are for authorized purposes.

XI. The Quartermaster will be held accountable for all property
purchased with the Prison Fund, and he will make a return of it to
the Commissary General of Prisoners at the end of each calendar
month, which will show the articles on hand on the first day of the
month; the articles purchased, issued, and expended during the
month; and the articles remaining on hand.   The return will be supported by abstracts of the articles purchased, issued, and expended,
certified by the Quartermaster, and approved by the Commanding
Officer.

XII. The Commanding Officer will cause requisitions to be made
by his Quartermaster for such clothing as may be absolutely necessary
for the prisoners, which requisition will be approved by him, after a
careful inquiry as to the necessity, and submitted for the approval of
the Commissary General of Prisoners.

The clothing will be issued by the Quartermaster to the prisoners,
with the assistance and under the supervision of an officer detailed for
the purpose, whose certificate that the issue has been made in his pres-

ence will be the Quartermaster's voucher for the clothing issued. From the 30th of April to the 1st of October, neither drawers nor socks will be allowed, except to the sick. When army clothing is issued, buttons and trimmings will be taken off the coats, and the skirts will be cut so short that the prisoners who wear them will not be mistaken for United States soldiers.

XIII. The Sutler for the prisoners is entirely under the control of the Commanding Officer, who will require him to furnish the prescribed articles, and at reasonable rates. For this privilege the Sutler will be taxed a small amount by the Commanding Officer, according to the amount of his trade, which tax will be placed in the hands of the Commissary to make part of the Prison Fund.

XIV. All money in possession of prisoners, or received by them, will be taken charge of by the Commanding Officer, who will give receipts for it to those to whom it belongs. Sales will be made to prisoners by the Sutler on orders on the Commanding Officer, which orders will be kept as vouchers in the settlement of the individual accounts. The Commanding Officer will procure proper books in which to keep an account of all moneys deposited in his hands, these accounts to be always subject to inspection by the Commissary General of Prisoners, or other inspecting officer. When prisoners are transferred from the post, the moneys belonging to them, with a statement of the amount due each, will be sent with them, to be turned over by the officer in charge to the officer to whom the prisoners are delivered, who will give receipts for the money. When prisoners are paroled, their money will be returned to them.

XV. All articles sent by friends to prisoners, if proper to be delivered, will be carefully distributed as the donors may request; such as are intended for the sick passing through the hands of the Surgeon, who will be responsible for their proper use. Contributions must be received by an officer, who will be held responsible that they are delivered to the person for whom they are intended. All uniform, clothing, boots, or equipments of any kind for military service, weapons of all kinds, and intoxicating liquors, including malt liquors, are among the contraband articles. The material for outer clothing should be gray, or some dark mixed color, and of inferior quality. Any excess of clothing, over what is required for immediate use, is contraband.

XVI. When prisoners are seriously ill, their nearest relatives, being loyal, may be permitted to make them short visits; but under no other circumstances will visitors be admitted without the authority of the Commissary General of Prisoners. At those places where the guard is inside the enclosure, persons having official business to transact with the Commander or other officer will be admitted for such purposes, but will not be allowed to have any communication with the prisoners.

XVII. Prisoners will be permitted to write and to receive letters, not to exceed one page of common letter paper each, provided the matter is strictly of a private nature. Such letters must be 'examined by a reliable non-commissioned officer, appointed for that purpose by the Commanding Officer, before they are forwarded or delivered to the prisoners.

XVIII. Prisoners who have been reported to the Commissary General of Prisoners will not be paroled or released except by authority of the Secretary of War.

W. HOFFMAN,

Col. 3d Infantry, Commissary General of Prisoners.

NOTE.

THE publishers have the names of all of those soldiers who perished at Andersonville, the date of death, and the number of their graves; and they contemplate publishing the list hereafter, if sufficient encouragement is offered.

Address   LEE & SHEPARD,

149 Washington Street, Boston.

LIST OF ILLUSTRATIONS.

The Illustrations were drawn by the author from sketches upon the spot, and from photographs which were taken by the rebels during the occupation of the prison. The figures are by Charles A. Barry, Esq., and the engraving by Henry Marsh, Esq.

INDEX.

BOOK FIRST.

BOOK SECOND.

BOOK THIRD.

BOOK FOURTH.

BOOK FIFTH.

BOOK SIXTH.

BOOK SEVENTH.

BOOK EIGHTH.

APPENDIX.

Boston Public Library
Central Library, Copley Square

Division of
Reference and Research Services

The Date Due Card in the pocket indicates the date on or before which this book should be returned to the Library.

Please do not remove cards from this pocket.